SLAB MARBLE SLEPT HERE

Commentaries by Vic Miller

Edited by Bruce Miller

Kook Radio broadcaster service award.

To my wife JoAnne for all her support over the years and to
Bruce and Sylvia for making the publishing of this book possible.

Miller, Vic
Slab Marble Slept Here - Commentaries by Vic Miller
1st Edition, by Vic Miller, Edited by Bruce Miller
ISBN: 9781955023153

Summary: Slab Slept Here features more than 100 of Vic Miller's 600+ commentaries, covering Billings and Montana topics to sports, politics, the lighter side of holidays and travel, and his 'where angels fear to tread' predictions for the coming year. His fictious friend Slab Marble plays a starring role in many of these favorite commentaries that aired on KTVQ-2 from 1991-2013.

Audience: All Ages.

Published by Green Kids Club, Inc., P.O. Box 50030, Idaho Falls, ID 83405

Foreword

Vic Miller wasn't the first person to provide radio or TV news to the state, but his presence and contributions over the decades have been so numerous and substantial that most people think of him first when his corner of the information/entertainment world is mentioned.

Consider the facts: Vic's career in news began in 1953, when he was hired to work at KOOK radio in Billings as an announcer and newscaster. In 1959, he moved to KOOK TV, now KTVQ, and served as news anchor, operations director and station general manager, a position he held for 18 years. He won several awards during his long career, including induction into the Montana Broadcasters Association Hall of Fame in 1998. And during this time, he also presented the weekly commentaries that became his most widely recognized and appreciated contributions to the public conversation—the very commentaries that are the focus of this book.

The art and skill involved in commentary writing should not be underestimated or taken for granted. Anyone who appreciated Andy Rooney's reflections on 60 Minutes will recognize the same memorable mix of humor, common sense, lucid language, and thought-provoking content in Vic's reflections. We personally have been fans of Vic's weekly appearances from the time they began until the last broadcast on December 26, 2013. While there is much to appreciate in the more than 600 essays, including their sheer number (talk about staying power!), perhaps what we admire most is their deftly even-handed, non-partisan approach: whether viewers are liberal or conservative or somewhere in between, they're unlikely to pigeonhole Vic politically, and everyone should find a bit of wisdom to agree with in any piece they read or listen to. Food for thought has never been so tastefully presented!

Deborah Schaffer, Ph.D.
Professor of English Emerita,
Montana State University Billings

Rachel Schaffer, Ph.D.
Professor of English Emerita,
Montana State University Billings

Table of Contents

Chapter 1 - Around the House 1
'Wallpaper' – 1991.. 2
'Leaf Raking' – 2002 3
'Some Assembly Required' – 2006 4
'Big Black Thing Revisited' – 2002 5
'Nail Gun' – 2000 6
'Victory Garden' – 2007 7
'Home Projects' – 2006 8
'Don't Bet on It' – 1994 9
'Snow Thrower' – 2013 10
'Christian Science and My Cut Thumb' – 1999 11
Chapter 2 - Montana...**12**
'Getting on a Horse (Centennial Cattle Drive)' – 1989... 13
'Butte Pigeons' - 2012 14
'New Montana Quarter' – 2005 15
'Poet Laureate' – 2004 16
'Wine Festival' – 2002 17
'Beer Drinkers' – 2010 18
'Yellowstone Earthquake' – 2009 19
'Cowboy Wardrobe' – 1989 20
'Montana History Test' – 2008 21
'Montana License Plates' – 2008 22
Chapter 3 - Holidays **23**
'Christmas Pageants' – 1999 24
'Christmas Poll' – 2003 25
'Christmas Shoppers' – 2007 26
'Slab Christmas Gifts' – 2006 27
'History of Halloween' – 2003 28
'Columbus Day' – 2012 29
'Groundhog Day' – 2002 30
New Year's Eve' - 1999 31
'Snerd Christmas Letter' – 2004 32
'Thanksgiving' – 2002 33
'Turkey Growers' – 1999 34
'Black and Blue Friday' – 2013 35
'Fruitcakes' – 2007 36
'St. Patrick's Day Swim' - 2001 37
'White Sulfur Springs 4th of July' – July 4, 2003 38
Chapter 4 - Grab Bag..**39**
'Lawrence Welk' – April 8, 2010 40
'Cloning Dolly the Sheep' - 1997 41
'Goat Chops' – 1999 42
'Jackrabbits' – 2008 43
'Mourning Doves' – 2005 44
'Not a Kid Anymore' – 2000 45
'Rock Scam' – 2004 46
'Running of the Bulls' – 2013 47
'Service Agreement' – 2006 48
'Siberian Tigers' – 2000 49
'Smoke' – 2000 50
'Standardized Stuff' – 2001 51
'Warning Labels' - 2001 52
'Graduation Commencement' - 2000 53

Chapter 5 - Observational **54**
'Academy Awards' – 2007 55
'Alleged' – 2003 56
'Crankers' – 2000 57
'Expiration Date' - 1990 58
'Fainting Goats' – 1990 59
'Legalized Gambling' – 2000 60
'Mars' – 2004 61
'Physical Checkup' – 2002 62
'Potbelly Pigs' - 1992 63
'Shorts' – 1997 64
'Street Crossing Buttons' – 2006 65
'Laws' – 2000 66
'8th Grade Education' – 2001 67
'Dinosaur Roar' - 1990 68
Chapter 6 - Politics & Taxes **69**
'Legislative Quiz' – 2003 70
'My Election Loss' - 1996 71
'President's Visit to Billings' – 2000 72
'Politically Correct' – 2009 73
'Clinton Wedding' – 2010 74
'Governor Marble' – 2003 75
'Montana Lullaby' – 2007 76
'Parliamentary Government' – 2001 77
'District Judge' – 2010 78
'Beer Tax' – 2003 79
Chapter 7 - Sports **80**
'Golf is Exercise' – 2000 81
'Olympics' – 2002 82
'Concussions' – 2010 83
'Fitness' – 2000 84
'Soccer' – 2002 85
'Summer Olympics' – 2009 86
'Super Bowl Halftime Show' – 2001 87
'Club Championship' – 2012 88
'Professional Golfers' - 1991 89
'Little League Baseball' – 2009 90
Chapter 8 - Travel **91**
'Bicycles' – 1999 92
'Canada Trip' – 2003 93
'Oregon Trip' - 2001 94
'Student Drivers' - 1997 95
'Winter in Yellowstone' – 2002 96
'Airplane Trip – 2005 97
'Australians' – 2004 98
'Cell Phones' – 2006 99
'Diagonal Parking' – 2002 100
'Parking Garage' – 2013 101
'Cadillac Smoke' – 2009 102
Chapter 9 - Where Angels Fear to Tread...........**103**
'1997 Predictions' – 1997 104
'2000 Predictions' - 1999 105
'2002 Predictions' – 2001 106
'2003 Predictions' – 2002 107
'2004 Predictions' – 2004 108
'2010 Predictions' – 2009 109
Last Commentary on Air - 2013 110
About the Author 112
PHOTOS 113

Introduction

This book contains some of the television commentaries I have done over the years. Given the fact I have done hundreds, this represents a small portion of them. I had no desire to have a book that rivaled War and Peace in length. Each commentary has been relatively short since I have never felt my role in life was to cure chronic cases of insomnia.

While some of my commentaries have dealt with serious topics, the vast majority are the result of having a warped sense of humor. When I was in radio a friend and I used to do fake interviews with people such as I.R. Literate, the president of Southern Montana College which had a ten-thousand seat football stadium with a shed out back for classrooms. Another guest was Slab Marble, an opinionated out of work philosopher.

Slab is the only one who moved with me from radio to television and continued to have the traits of a number of people I have known who march to the beat of a different drum. At the moment, he is trying to recall why he is wearing his baseball cap on backwards.

I hope you enjoy the book.

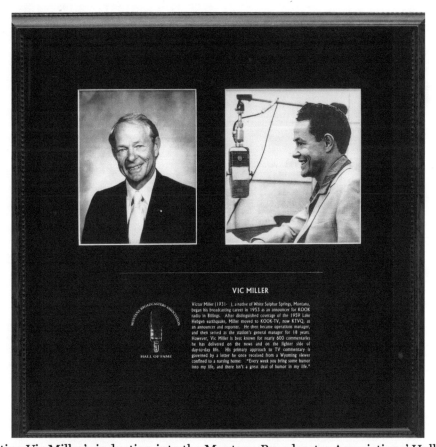

Plaque commemorating Vic Miller's induction into the Montana Broadcaster Associations' Hall of Fame in 1998.

Chapter 1
AROUND THE HOUSE

"Now I know how Dr. Frankenstein must have felt.
We both spent a great deal of time and effort
creating something, only to discover
that there's a good chance our creations
are going to attempt to kill us."

- Vic Miller

Chapter 1 - Around the House

'Wallpaper' – February 14, 1991

I was going to talk about the accomplishments of the 1991 Montana Legislature, but the commentary would have been shorter than Gus Koernig's introduction, so I've decided to talk about wallpaper.

My wife and I hung some wallpaper awhile back. We do this about every 20-years, which is about the right interval between wallpaper hangings.

It should be noted that there are two kinds of wallpaper. There is the kind without a distinctive pattern, which is relatively easy to work with, and there is the kind with wood nymphs chasing butterflies across a flowered meadow, which is the kind you always seem to end up buying. Matching the pattern on wood nymph wallpaper is virtually impossible to do.

Frankly, I've never looked upon the fact that the pattern doesn't exactly match as being any big deal. The truth of the matter is, we might even have one panel of wallpaper where the wood nymphs are seemingly defying the law of gravity, and I'm not going to get too emotional about it. However, for some reason it concerns my wife to the point where she's been known to insist we take the panel off and hang it right side up.

To make matters worse, when I figure we're done, she sometimes points out places where she claims the wallpaper has bubbles the size of hot air balloons, and wrinkles that bring back memories of Phyllis Diller before she had her facelift. Not only that, she has the audacity to suggest we actually do something about what I consider to be these insignificant flaws.

If you want to put your marriage to the test, go out and buy some wallpaper. If you make it through the project without threatening to kill each other, you have a pretty good relationship.

Chapter 1 - Around the House

'Leaf Raking' – September 26, 2002

There's enough bad news floating around these days without me pointing out more of it. On the other hand, I certainly don't want to be accused of suppressing the news. Therefore, I am here to inform you that summer is history. I realize, that this year there was only a two week period between Memorial Day and Labor Day, and I certainly hope either the FBI or the CIA is checking into who hijacked summer.

Be that as it may, we are now experiencing fall. This was obvious when I watched a couple of leaves fall off one of our trees. This brought home the fact we have a serious problem confronting us, which is why I want all of you men to pay close attention. The end of summer is a bummer, but leaves falling off trees borders on the catastrophic. These leaves have to be raked up and disposed of, and the problem facing husbands is determining the best way to break the news to our wives that it's almost leaf raking time.

A rookie husband who hasn't been through one of these leaf raking skirmishes would probably deal with the problem in a practical and logical manner. He would cheerfully point out to his bride that by raking the leaves, she would maintain the fine muscle tone she developed over the summer pushing the lawnmower, and leaf raking will go a long way toward insuring that she won't develop sore muscles this winter when the time comes for her to shovel the snow off the driveway.

Battle scarred veterans of the leaf raking wars, are fully aware that this would be a major tactical error that could have life threatening consequences. They would be quick to point out that this approach should never be used unless you relish the thought of a quick trip to the hospital emergency room to have a rake handle removed from your ear.

At this point I suppose all of you husbands expect me to tell you how to go about getting your wives to handle the leaf raking chores in a way that doesn't involve you're ending up in the back of an ambulance. Unfortunately, I haven't a clue. I feel I've already done my bit by alerting you of the impending crisis and from here on out its every male chauvinist pig for himself.

'Some Assembly Required' – March 30, 2006

My wife went shopping the other day and came home with five-foot high cabinet that had a couple of drawers, some shelves and two doors. It looked very nice. At least the picture of it on the box looked very nice.

Yes, it came in a box. It seems like almost everything comes in a box these days, even wine, although that's a different commentary.

The cabinet in question required assembly and had a dreaded instruction sheet. I'm like most other males who will drive around in a vehicle until it runs out of gas rather than stop and ask someone for directions, and I also feel it is an insult to my manhood to have to refer to an instruction sheet when assembling something.

The one time I attempted to follow the instructions turned out to be a very frustrating experience given the fact the instructions contained a lot of technical stuff advising me to attach part "A" to part "C" using Cam "B" and Cam Bolt "J". It doesn't help when I am getting ready to try to assemble something that I discover I'm going to need a Phillips screwdriver. I never have a problem finding about fifteen blade screwdrivers, but all of my Phillips screwdrivers appear to have gone south.

In any event, I managed to get the cabinet assembled ands it looks just fine although as is usually the case, I had a few extra parts left over. I'm convinced the people at the factory have a weird sense of humor and always toss in a few extra parts just to confuse me.

As I was getting ready to throw away the instruction sheet, which I hadn't used, I did happen to notice that at the top of the sheet in very bold print was the word WARNING. I discovered it was warning me that when fully assembled, the cabinet could tip over on me.

Now I know how Dr. Frankenstein must have felt. We both spent a great deal of time and effort creating something, only to discover that there's a good chance our creations are going to attempt to kill us.

At the present time, the cabinet is standing tall against one of our walls and thus far hasn't displayed any aggressive tendencies. However, I know better than to turn my back on it.

'Big Black Thing Revisited' – May 2, 2002

A couple of years ago I did a commentary about the big black thing the city gave me to put my trash in and how pleased I was with it. Every Monday morning, I put the big black thing full of trash out by the back gate and every Monday evening when I retrieved it, it was empty. My trash problem for the week was solved; I didn't have to fill out a lot of stupid forms or stand in an endless line.

I mentioned that it was the one aspect of government, local, state or national, that I was completely happy with.

However, something happened recently that put a strain on our relationship. I was emptying a wastebasket into the big black thing before dragging it out to the back gate, when a gust of wind came up and the lid came down and whacked me on the head. This prompted me to say something like "Goodness that was painful." I immediately blamed myself for never getting around to reading the warning label on the big black thing. I figured that had I read the warning label, it would undoubtedly have cautioned me not to open the lid and attempt to put something in it if I was pregnant or if the wind was blowing.

I was then shocked to discover the big black thing didn't have a warning label. Nothing to alert me that the object that I had always looked upon as being docile might turn on me and whack me on the head.

At this point I figured I'd better call my lawyer, Algonquin J. Calhoun, and see if he got his license back after being disbarred following that unfortunate incident with the goat.

However, I was beginning to get a lump on my head where the lid of the big black thing had whacked me. I recalled you are supposed to put something cold on it to reduce the swelling, so I decided to hold a cold beer against it. After the swelling went down, I figured as long as I was holding the beer I might as well drink it and didn't get around to calling Algonquin.

That doesn't mean that I have ruled out suing the city for pain and suffering, although being a reasonable man, I am willing to settle out of court.

'Nail Gun' – February 17, 2000

The other day l saw my friend Slab Marble coming out of the Cooked in Lard Café and asked him how things were going. Slab said things weren't going all that well. He said his life started to turn into a moldy prune right after he purchased an electric nail gun. He said he decided to buy the thing after he had hit his thumb with a hammer half a dozen times while trying to build a bookcase.

I said I did notice the thumb on his left hand resembled a penny that had been run over by a railroad train, so buying an electric nail gun was probably a good idea.

Slab said I was wrong and it had turned out to be a terrible idea. He said he was afraid to use it after reading all of the warnings. For example, he said the instructions warned him not to use the thing if he was under the influence of alcohol, and if he had to choose between the nail gun and a can of whatever beer was on sale that week, the gun would never fire a nail.

He also said the instruction sheet warned him that he should wear snug-fitting clothing instead of loose clothing while operating the nail gun. Slab said he had kind of a loose body so he liked to wear loose clothing. He said he had serious reservations about putting on a pair of leotards just to nail two boards together. He also said the instructions advised him to keep children, animals, and bystanders away from the work area while using the nail gun. I agreed that could be a problem since the sight of him in a pair of leotards was likely to draw a big crowd.

Then he said that on top of everything else, the instructions advised him to wear rubber gloves while operating the nail gun and that he didn't have any rubber gloves. I told him the next time he went in for his physical checkup, maybe he could ask the doctor to give him the rubber glove after the doctor was done with it.

Slab started to walk away, saying he should have known better than to expect sympathy from me. I told him sympathy was my middle name and I'd be the first one to send him a get well card after he shot himself in the foot with the nail gun.

Chapter 1 - Around the House

'Victory Garden' – August 9, 2007

The other day someone asked me if we grew a vegetable garden. When we first moved into our home, we did have a garden but then the trees on our property got so big there was too much shade to grow vegetables.

This is not to say that I haven't had a great deal of experience when it comes to gardening. When I was an urchin growing up in a small Montana town during World War II, all kids were encouraged to grow a Victory Garden. For the benefit of those in the audience who flunked history, World War II took place after World War I.

But getting back to my Victory Garden, to get us launched there was a gathering of my grade school class. We were given some basic instructions about gardening, and I was elected President of our Victory Garden Club. We never got around to having another meeting. There's a lot to be said for that. If every Congressional or Legislative Committee had an initial meeting and never met again, we might all be better off.

Having a Victory Garden was an educational experience. I learned that if something in a garden looks green and healthy, the odds are it is a weed. Other things I learned included the fact that vegetables planted too close together take great joy in strangling each other, and that nothing makes a garden look really large as gazing at it while holding a hoe in your hand.

While it pains me to admit it, as far as my Victory Garden was concerned, it was not what you could call an unqualified success. Everything that wasn't a weed came under heavy attack from insects. I finally capitulated and ran up the white flag in early July, although I felt guilty knowing my Victory Garden crop failure could very well influence the outcome of World War II. For several months, I lived in fear that General Patton might stop by and slap me for shirking my duty.

Every once in a while, the thought crosses my mind that it would be nice to have a garden again, but fortunately the thought soon passes. It's a lot easier to go to the farmers market, plunk down a few bucks, and enjoy fresh vegetables without ever having to hoe a weed.

Chapter 1 - Around the House

'Home Projects' – January 4, 2006

I hadn't heard from my friend Slab Marble for a while, so I thought I'd give him a call. Slab said he'd been kind of busy since his wife insisted that he take care of some home projects he'd been postponing for a little while. I asked what constituted a little while, and he said since 1996.

Slab explained that back then everyone was predicting the world would end when the year 2000 rolled around, so he figured there was no reason to do a lot of stuff with the end of the world just around the corner. He said after 2000 came and nothing happened, he just never got inspired to do the stuff. He said his wife got him inspired by threatening to quit cooking unless he got in gear.

I asked what his latest project was and he said he'd put a thing on the roof so the vent on top of the kitchen stove would have some place for the exhaust to go. He said he went to the store and bought the thing for the roof and some flexible pipe, and then went up and sawed a hole in the roof.

I said I was surprised to hear that, as I recalled he had a roof with a rather high pitch and he'd always had a fear of heights. Slab said the roof's so steep that every time he's up there he expects to encounter a Sherpa guide and half a dozen mountain climbers who reached the peak and are on their way down. He said being on the roof scared him to death but he eventually got the thing installed. Slab he was so happy to get down he was almost glad he went up.

I told him that I'd noticed that about everything I buy these days seems to be made in China and asked if this was the case with the stuff he'd used on his project. Slab said he was surprised to discover the thing for the roof was made in Mexico. He said judging from all the news stories he'd been hearing about the Mexican border, it was probably the only thing to make it across the border all year that wasn't an illegal alien. I told him that was a politically sensitive subject, and Slab said he was a politically insensitive kind of guy.

Chapter 1 - Around the House

'Don't Bet on It' – April 14, 1994

We had a death in the family last weekend. Our dearly beloved hot water heater passed-away at the tender age of seven years. Its predecessor lived to the ripe old age of ten years before expiring, but I've found that almost every time I've replaced something, the replacement never lasts as long as the thing it is replacing.

A few years ago, I had to put in a new motor to run the fan on our furnace. The old motor was at least twenty years old before it cashed in its chips. When buying a new motor, I mentioned to the guy that I hoped it would last as long as the old one. He replied, "Don't bet on it.' I'm glad I didn't. That motor only lasted three years. One year longer than the warranty.

Anyway, last weekend our hot water heater started making some Mount Vesuvius sounds and water began coming out of places where water was not supposed to come out. I was forced to administer last rites and turn off its water supply.

In addition to the fact, replacements don't last as long as the things they are replacing, it is also a fact of life that replacements always cost more than the things they are replacing. I suppose if I were a real Joe Fixit, I would have purchased a new hot water heater and installed it myself, saving a lot of money.

However, while I have no problem with do-it-yourself projects involving electricity, I make it a practice of not messing with things involving natural gas. I always have this vision of hearing a big boom, followed by me and the hot water tank being launched into outer space. I don't mind a little adventure in my life, but it's never been one of my goals to be the first person on our block to take an unscheduled spacewalk.

We had someone come over with a new water heater and he did a nice job of installing it. I didn't mention to him that I hoped it would last as long as the last one. I was afraid he might say, "Don't bet on it."

Chapter 1 - Around the House

'Snow Thrower' – November 7, 2013

I called my friend Slab Marble the other day and reminded him that I'd let him borrow my snow thrower last winter after he'd told me he was having a problem with his, although he'd neglected to mention that the snow thrower he was having trouble with a was his wife.

Slab said he'd probably been in a state of shock because for some unknown reason his wife had refused to continue shoveling the driveway even though he'd reminded her it helped her keep the fine muscle tone she developed from raking leaves, and she'd be in good shape when it was time for her to mow the lawn again.

I told him that was all very interesting, but now that winter is getting ready to bushwhack us again, I needed my snow thrower. Slab said he'd been meaning to call and tell me about a funny thing that had happened.

He said he had a lot of leaves in his yard and given the episode with his wife he had been somewhat hesitant about inquiring about when she was going to get around to raking them up.

Then he figured that the snow thrower had done such a good job of blowing snow he would use it to blow all the leaves in his yard over to his neighbor's yard since his neighbor wasn't home at the time. Slab said things were working out as planned except he forgot the hose was buried under the leaves. When the snow thrower hit the hose, there was this banging sound and pieces of my snow blower flew all over the place.

Slab said since my call was about getting my snow thrower back, he'd be happy to return it. That way, people wouldn't see that piece of junk in his yard and assume it belonged to him.

Chapter 1 - Around the House

'Christian Science and My Cut Thumb' – October 14, 1999

In the process of moving my office from the TV station to our home, I discovered what I perceived to be the need to move an electrical outlet to a more convenient location. I did not regard this as being in the same category as brain surgery, since I had performed similar transplants a number of times.

However, in the process of stripping some insulation off a wire, the knife slipped, and I ended up stripping the insulation off my left thumb. At this point the smart thing to do would have been to go to the emergency room and have my thumb stitched up. Of course, an even smarter thing would have been to avoid carving up my thumb in the first place, so it was obvious that I was not into doing smart things that particular day.

In my infinite wisdom, I decided to skip the emergency room and used kind of a modified Christian Science approach. I stopped the bleeding, put a really big Band-Aid on the thumb, told it to heal itself, and played a round of golf that afternoon.

The thumb appeared to be complying with my request, but then complications set in, so I decided to have someone take a look at it whose medical training was more extensive than the first aid class I took back in the sixth grade.

They took some x-rays, gave me some antibiotics, and bandaged the thumb. It now seems to be healing, although I still have to re-bandage it every day.

I'll have to admit, I am not quite as good at doing the bandage thing as the lady at the Billings Clinic. My bandaging job looks like something you might see on the hand of a just revived mummy in a horror movie.

The sight of this weird bandage causes some folks to get alarmed, back away, and ask if it's something serious. I had to reassure them that there is no need for alarm because, like modern art, it's not really as bad as it looks.

It has been said that just about everything in life is a learning experience, and that brings us to what I learned from this, other than the fact I may not be cut out to be a Christian Scientist. What I learned is, if the matter comes up again, instead of attempting to move an electrical outlet box and running the risk of doing further damage to my anatomy, I will go out and buy a really long extension cord and use the existing electrical outlet.

After all, a house doesn't have to fall on me, although at the rate I'm going, I wouldn't rule it out.

Chapter 2
MONTANA

"Someone suggested I should be in the
[Montana] cattle drive and my brother-in-law
would probably loan a horse to me.
My brother-in-law is a great guy, but he has a
lively sense of humor, so I'd probably end up
with a horse named "Slam Dunk"
or "Rocket Launcher."

- Vic Miller

Chapter 2 - Montana

'Getting on a Horse (Centennial Cattle Drive)' – August 10, 1989

The other day my colleague, Taylor Brown, told me that I should be in the Great Montana Centennial Cattle Drive, and even offered to loan a horse to me. He assured me that it was a gentle animal that his kid rides all the time, but I have a feeling that the moment I got on it, the horse would undergo a personality change and start acting like it belonged in Dale Small's bucking horse string.

A few weeks ago, I was in Joliet and someone suggested I should be in the cattle drive and allowed that my brother-in-law would probably loan a horse to me. My brother-in-law is a great guy, but he has a lively sense of humor, so I'd probably end up with a horse named "Slam Dunk" or "Rocket Launcher".

It's been about 20 years since I have been on a horse and riding 10 miles a day for 6 days could be a painful experience, which may surprise those of you who thought all broadcasters were numb from the ears both ways.

I think the cattle drive is a great idea and wish them well, but while I support it, I'm not ready to sacrifice my body by getting on a horse. I don't care if it is the way Clint Eastwood got his start.

Chapter 2 - Montana

'Butte Pigeons' - August 9, 2012

I had a call from my friend Slab Marble and he said as he recalled I was an expert on pigeons. I replied I wasn't sure about being an expert, but when I was a kid, I did raise pigeons. Milt Mayn and I became interested in pigeons and on occasion Milt's dad would drive us to Helena and buy us some pigeons from a guy who was in the pigeon raising business. These were acrobatic pigeons known as rollers and tumblers. Rollers would be flying like normal pigeons and then do a back flip and keep on flying. Tumblers would climb up in the air and then start tumbling, going end over end until they almost reached the ground and then pull out of it.

Slab then said that given my background I should go over to Butte and give the folks the benefit of my expertise. I told him he must be confused because, as I recalled the only tumblers and rollers I had ever heard of as residing in Butte, were guys who were tossed out of the M&M Bar on St Patrick's Day.

Slab said he wasn't confused and that Butte has some big time problems with pigeons. He said there apparently are a lot of pigeons in Butte that have set up housekeeping in buildings that don't have windows. I told him that given Butte's reputation for their mild winters I could see why people wouldn't bother spending a lot of money putting in windows they didn't need.

Slab said he was talking about uninhabited buildings and, when the pigeons are not camped out there, they can be found all over town and folks are getting tired of all the pigeon poop. He said in the old days the rugged individuals in Butte would have declared war on the invaders and the battle would have been over in a week, but now they've become civilized and have decided to spend thousands of dollars to conduct a study. I told him it suddenly occurred to me that he had been correct when he called me an expert on pigeons, and if the citizens of Butte were to offer me several thousand bucks, I'd be more than happy to go over and conduct a study.

Chapter 2 - Montana

'New Montana Quarter' – July 14, 2005

I had a call from my friend Slab Marble the other day and he sounded real excited and asked if I had heard the news. I told him I didn't have the foggiest idea what he was referring to and Slab said there is going to be a new Montana commemorative quarter and Montana Governor Schwarzenegger was asking people to send in their ideas for possible designs.

I told him I had heard about the new quarter, but the governor of Montana was not Arnold Schwarzenegger, it was Brian Schweitzer. Slab said in that case he must have gone to the polls in the last election and voted for the wrong guy, but the important thing is that we are going to have this neat new commemorative quarter and he had this great idea for the new design. I knew I'd live to regret it, but I asked him to tell me about it.

Slab said we need a real stud muffin quarter and given the fact that he is the epitome of what a real Montanan looks like, on one side of the coin would be a portrait of him, not the way he looks now but back when he had a lot of hair. He said on the other side of the coin would be a scene where a chubby little tourist with a camera, is being chased across a meadow by an angry mama moose, and in the background would be some good old boys standing around laughing and scratching and drinking cans of whatever beer was on sale that week while enjoying the proceedings.

I told him it was my understanding that the governor has decided that no person, living or dead will be allowed on the new coin, and furthermore the coin can't include anything that might be construed as being frivolous or inappropriate. Slab said that was the dumbest thing he had ever heard of, and that kind of thinking will probably result in us ending up with an insipid quarter that'll be about as popular as a Susan B. Anthony dollar.

I told him I wasn't the one who made the rules and Slab said he was going to call up Montana Governor Schwarzenegger and give him a piece of his mind. I refrained from pointing out he didn't have any pieces to spare.

'Poet Laureate' – January 13, 2004

My friend Slab Marble called and said he wanted me to be the first to know that he is going to be the new poet laureate for the state of Montana. I thanked him for sharing that with me and confessed that it was news to me that we even had a poet laureate and I was somewhat surprised that he had been chosen for the job.

Slab said at the moment we don't have a poet laureate and they haven't actually announced his selection yet, but hearing me imply he might not be qualified to be poet laureate showed how little I knew of his long association with cultural stuff like poetry. He added that for my information he has long been an admirer those famous American poets, Jack Frost and Carl Sandbag. I admitted that I wasn't much of an expert on American poets but I thought the name of the two people he was referring to was actually Robert Frost and Carl Sandburg.

Slab accused me of nitpicking and that being overly concerned about minor details has been known to shut off the flow of creative juices in poets like him. He then advised me that a couple of state senators are on record as saying what Montana needs is a poet laureate. I said I thought what Montana needed was more good paying jobs, and Slab said I was one of the reasons culture is having such a tough time getting a toehold in the state.

I told him he could be right, and then asked him why he felt he was qualified to be Montana's poet laureate. Slab said that when he was in grade school he had his friends in stitches when he recited one of his poems. He said for example there was the one that started, "There once was a man from ....I cut him off and said that while limericks like this might have had them rolling in the aisles in grade school, I wasn't sure that's what the senators were looking for in a state poet laureate.

Slab said he was convinced that's exactly what they are looking for and would soon realize he was the only man for the job. I had to admit that his being named poet laureate probably wouldn't be the most bizarre thing that's likely to happen in Helena this year.

Chapter 2 - Montana

'Wine Festival' – June 6, 2002

I ran into my friend Slab Marble the other day and asked him if he had done anything exciting recently. Slab said he went to the MSU-Billings wine festival. I told him that it was the last thing I would have expected from a guy who is noted for buying whatever beer is on sale that week.

Slab said he had been at a gathering and one of the people there had accused him of being uncouth. Slab said he told her she was wrong and that he had couth coming out of his ears and the woman said that was hair.

He said at that point he decided maybe he'd better brush up on being an urban sophisticate and he thought a good way to start was to attend the wine festival and learn some of the neat terms that he could toss around and impress people.

I said given the fact he has always referred to wines as the white stuff and the red stuff, it must have been a rather steep learning curve.

Slab said they did have some strange ways of describing different wines. He said one was described as being a ripe, robust wine that explodes in the mouth and has a tremendous balance of flinty acids. He said the last time he felt that something had exploded in his mouth was when he went down to Mexico and ordered a bowl of their extra hot chili. He said he decided not to try that wine.

He said another wine was described as exceptional with soft, velvety plump flavors that complement pleasing aromas of violets, plums, leather and tobacco. He said he passed on this one too. He also told me they auctioned off some wines for more than a thousand bucks, which is more than he paid to have his septic tank put in.

I asked him if he came away from the wine festival feeling like a new man and he said he had a good time and picked up some handy words to use at cocktail parties. He said when he starts tossing around phrases like opulent finish, voluptuously textured, complimentary acidity, and incredible complexity, people will realize they are in the presence of a man of great couth.

He said attending the wine festival could prove to be the best money he ever spent, with the exception of the septic tank.

Chapter 2 - Montana

'Beer Drinkers' – April 1, 2010

I called my friend Slab Marble the other day and asked him if he had heard the news. Slab said he hadn't gotten much news lately since his TV is on the blink and the only thing he can get is the cartoon channel.

I told him the Beer Institute recently announced that Montana was the top beer drinking state in the nation in 2008 and the 2009 figures should be available in the near future. Slab said the people at the Beer Institute were probably nursing hangovers and were running a little behind.

I said he might be right but the fact is, we were number one in 2008 and that the average Montanan over twenty-one drank 43.5 gallons of beer.

Slab asked how this compares with how we've done in the past and I told him the Beer Institute only showed figures for 2003 when we were on fourth place, with Nevada coming in number one that year. Slab said Nevada has a built in advantage since it gets so hot down there it makes people demented, and they probably get up every morning and pour a gallon of beer over their corn flakes.

I noted the other places that beat us out in 2003 were North Dakota and New Hampshire. Slab said he spent a week in North Dakota once and ended up drinking about ten gallons of beer all by himself just for something to do, and New Hampshire is where they always hold the first Presidential Primary with about a thousand candidates walking around lowering property values. He said that's enough to drive anyone to drink so he can understand why residents there hoist quite a few.

I told him I was somewhat shocked to learn that the average Montanan drank 43 gallons of beer each year and Slab said he was too, and thought it would be around 100, so there must be a lot of slackers out there, counting on him to keep us competitive. He said one person hurting our average is his neighbor who is 91 and she only kills a six-pack every two weeks. I said when the 2009 figures come out, if we are no longer number one, he may want to give her a good talking to. Slab said I could count on it.

Chapter 2 - Montana

'Yellowstone Earthquake' – August 20, 2009

On the evening of August 17, 1959, one of the severest earthquakes ever recorded on the North American continent hit an area by Hebgen Lake, near Yellowstone Park.

I was the news director of KOOK Radio in Billings at the time and the next day we chartered a plane from Lynch Flying service and flew to the site.

As we neared the quake area, we could see places where large portions of highway had dropped several feet for a distance of up to a hundred yards. There were a number of spots with green circles showing where springs were located. The water coming from these springs was the color of coffee with cream in it.

Flying up the Madison valley, we could see where a large part of a mountain had slid into the river valley, covering a portion of a popular campground and damming up the Madison River, forming what is now Quake Lake.

The quake had caused a tidal wave to splash over the dam at Hebgen Lake and there was concern the dam could collapse, flooding downstream communities. Fortunately, the dam held.

The West Yellowstone airport was small with no control tower. There were dozens of planes and helicopters coming and going, but our pilot found an opening and landed the plane. An Air Force helicopter had just brought in four survivors from the disaster area. I talked with an elderly couple who survived by climbing a tree as water behind the landslide continued to rise. They managed to hang on, but water was up to their necks when people in a boat rescued them the next morning. The woman said she was grateful to be alive, and praised the Lord's mercy. Survivors talked of boulders as large as automobiles bouncing past and wiping out everything in their path. They told of people screaming and calling out for help.

It was the first big story I had covered, and the CBS Radio Network carried three of my reports.

The earthquake killed 28 people and the bodies of more than half of them were never recovered. These included two Billings residents, Bernie and Inez Boynton. I did not know them, but in 1969, my wife and I purchased the home where we still live. We later learned that in 1959, it had been the home of the Boynton's, before they left on that ill-fated outing.

'Cowboy Wardrobe' – July 6, 1989

I've got a pair of Levi's and a couple western shirts so I figured I could pick up a few accessories and be all set for the Montana Centennial. Fortunately, my copy of the "Commemorative Edition of the Montana Centennial Official Products" catalog arrived just in time.

I find I can purchase a centennial custom cowboy hat with the "Montana crease" that makes it look like the wearer was hit over the head with an axe handle at the cost of only $150. A pair of centennial boots go for just $500, and centennial spurs that I can put on my boots and go jingle jangle, sell for $225. There is a neat silver centennial belt buckle that can be purchased for $225 and it will look nice with my $25 centennial belt.

To complete my centennial wardrobe, I can get a faithful reproduction of one of those dusters found in Charlie Russell paintings. They must have me in mind since the ad says it's "tailored for a contemporary cowboy." It sells for $135.

So, as you can see, if you really want to go western in a centennial way, it's pretty easy. Just get yourself a pair of Levi's, a western shirt and $1,260 worth of accessories. I can almost guarantee, that every time you wear this stuff, people will stop what they're doing, gaze at you, and say in wonderment, "there's another one of those clowns trying to impersonate a cowboy".

Montana History Test' – November 20, 2008

Someone, I believe it was either Socrates or Dave Barry, once said that a nation that does not know its history is not going to do well on the Scholastic Aptitude Test.

In order to discover how much, or how little, young people know about history, I periodically give tests. This one will not deal with world history or American history, just Montana history. The only people eligible to participate are those who are still in school. That includes Hubert Snodgrass who misbehaved in class and was sent down to the principal's office. Everyone forgot about him, and he has been there for the past twenty years and now has tenure. However, I digress. It is time for the test. Montana became a state in:

A. 1492

B. 1776

C. 1889

Montana has only had one woman governor. Her name is:

A. Calamity Jane

B. Hillary Clinton

C. Judy Martz

Montana's Official State Flower is:

A. The dandelion

B. The bitterroot

C. Aunt Jemima's pancake flour

In front of the capitol building in Helena, there is a statue of a person on a horse. That person is:

A. Don Quixote

B. Thomas Meagher

C. Lady Godiva

Finally, every two years the Montana legislature meets to:

A. Pass bills

B. Pass the buck

C. Pass gas

And there you have it. To see how you did on the test send me your answers along with a ten-dollar bill to handle shipping and handling. Actually, there is no shipping and handling involved, but given the performance of the stock market lately, I need the money.

Chapter 2 - Montana

'Montana License Plates' – March 13, 2008

Those of you who have lived in Montana for a few decades will recall that the state used to put out new automobile license plates about as often as Catholics elect a new Pope. And while other states had sophisticated slogans on their vehicle plates such as Idaho's "Famous Potatoes," Montana vehicle license plates read, "Prison Made."

While our plates looked old and dilapidated much of the time, with a slogan that was somewhat less than awe inspiring, the one thing that could be said about them was when you saw one you knew it was a Montana license plate. Now there are so many different Montana license plates you don't know if the vehicle is from Montana, Rhode Island, or Mars.

In addition to the standard plate that the state issues, there are an untold number of specialty plates. At times, it seems as if every entity in Montana has its own specialty plate. For example, there are 19 different license plates associated with Montana universities and colleges. Zoo Montana has a license plate as does Trout Unlimited, Ducks Unlimited, Rotary Club, Montana Cowboy Hall of Fame, and the Montana Spay/Neuter Task Force.

The vehicle in front of you might sport a license plate touting the Montana Right to Life Educational Trust, while the vehicle behind you could have a plate for Planned Parenthood of Montana. The Montana State Golf Association has a plate, as does the Havre Wrestling Club. Other entities with specialty plates include the Boy Scouts, the Girl Scouts, the FFA Foundation, the Montana 4-H foundation, and the Slab Marble Pink Plastic Flamingo Bird Sanctuary. OK, that last one hasn't surfaced yet.

In order for a group to get their own specialty plate, they have to give the state $4,000 up front, or file, with the Montana Motor Vehicle Department, a minimum of 400 prepaid applications for the sponsoring organizations plates. When a specialty plate is purchased, the group gets part of the proceeds. In theory, the plates can be a moneymaker for the organization, but as a number of entities have discovered to their dismay, if you put up your four grand and only sell a few plates, this endeavor is not going to have a happy ending.

It's obvious we've come a long way since the days of "Prison Made."

Chapter 3
HOLIDAYS

"If it weren't for Halloween and trick or treat,
it's safe to say most of these tycoons probably
wouldn't have been exposed to greed
until they entered kindergarten."

- Vic Miller

Chapter 3 - Holidays

'Christmas Pageants' – December 16, 1999

Back when the crust of the earth was cooling and I was in grade school, there were things called Christmas pageants. I don't know if they have Christmas pageants anymore. These days they probably have Holiday pageants where the reindeer talk about proper nutrition and Mrs. Santa Claus lectures the elves on being politically correct, cautioning them that under certain circumstances, those that even mention the meaning of Christmas can bring on the threat of a lawsuit.

But back in the dark ages when we were unenlightened about these things, someone in the policy making end of our grade school determined that there would be a Christmas pageant. They also determined that the cast would be composed of reluctant young urchins, none of whom were in the policy making end of the organization.

In looking over the parts, I decided that one of the plum roles would be that of a wise man. You didn't have to be a future Rhodes scholar to figure out that being a wise man was certainly a much better role than being one of the animals in the manger scene. This was strictly a low budget pageant and, being a manger animal meant that someone would put a dusty old rug over you, and you stood around, hunched over, trying not to sneeze.

Unfortunately, the teacher assigning the roles failed to recognize my potential so instead of being cast as a wise man, I was relegated to being the third shepherd from the right. However, she assured me that mine would be a speaking role. When pressed as to how many lines I would have, she told me my speaking role would consist of saying, "Hark." I said, "Hark, that's it? My speaking role wasn't even a two syllable word?"

She then advised me that if I would prefer to play the part of a manger animal, she was sure she could find another dusty old rug.

I told her that on second thought, I suddenly realized that being able to play the role of the third shepherd from the right, and having the opportunity to say "hark", was something I'd always wanted to do.

In thinking back, for the first few years I was in grade school I was small for my age and had a rather high voice. I guess I'm lucky the teacher assigning the roles didn't make me put on a pink bathrobe and play the part of Mary.

Chapter 3 - Holidays

'Christmas Poll' – December 18, 2003

It is now the moment many of you have all been waiting for, the results of our 2003 Christmas poll. I guess it's possible that some of you were not even aware that our Christmas poll took place but I'm sure the same could be said for a lot of other polls. No one knows about them until the results are announced. In our case we had a limited number of responses since we called people on the telephone between one and three in the morning, and for some unknown reason many of the folks who answered the phone uttered phrases that were not at all in keeping with the spirit of the season, and then hung up.

Since we had a limited number of responses the sampling error was plus or minus 75%, which I don't look upon as being any big deal.

First of all, we asked people to rate Santa Claus job performance. 51% approved of the job that Santa was doing. 35% disapproved of the job Santa was doing, claiming the rich were receiving more expensive gifts than the poor. 14% of the respondents thought that Santa Claus was a candidate seeking the presidential nomination and said they couldn't rate his job performance since at this point, he just wanted the job, but didn't actually have it.

Then we asked the people how they felt about reindeer. 60% felt they should be re-introduced into Yellowstone Park. 30% said they had no problem with reindeer as long as they didn't come into their backyards and eat the rose bushes. Almost 10% said there should be an open season on them, adding there should also be an open season on drivers who don't wait their turn at four way stop intersections. One respondent said she once went on a blind date with someone who looked a lot like a reindeer, and one said he had been served reindeer meat once and it tasted like pond scum. However, he later admitted he might have it confused with the time he had lutefisk.

For those of you who didn't have an opportunity to participate in the poll and want to be included next year, just let us know. However, before allowing you to participate, we first need a sworn statement promising that under no circumstances will you ever send us a fruitcake as a Christmas present.

Chapter 3 - Holidays

'Christmas Shoppers' – December 20, 2007

I'm starting to give some thought about getting started on my Christmas shopping. I realize it's not even Christmas Eve yet and there's no reason to panic, but I thought I might get started a little early this year.

I know you'll find this hard to believe, but there are some people who get started thinking about Christmas shopping even before me. I have even encountered some people who gave all the outward appearances of being perfectly normal until all of a sudden, they blurted out that they have their Christmas shopping completed by July.

By July, for heaven's sake. In July, the hot Christmas items haven't even surfaced that everyone will want but can't get because the stores guessed wrong and only ordered three of them. In July, I haven't even gotten around to returning the sweater I received last Christmas that turned out to be so large that it would even look baggy on Ted Kennedy.

Us real Americans can't get into Christmas shopping in July. We are out there golfing and fishing, and blowing off various body parts with firecrackers, and doing all of the other fun things you do in July. Santa doesn't show up at a department store until the middle of August and television stations don't even begin running Christmas commercials until Labor Day.

There is no doubt in my mind that people who have all their Christmas shopping done by July are an even greater threat to our way of life than global warming, or the 175 presidential candidates who are currently wandering around, acting weird and scaring the heck out of us. These early shoppers must be dealt with in a most severe manner to prevent the practice of spreading.

I have a proposal that all nine lawyers wearing robes and doing business as the United States Supreme Court will probably claim prevention of extra early Christmas shopping is cruel and unusual punishment, but desperate times call for desperate measures. Going back to something I suggested a number of years ago, I would like to see anyone caught Christmas shopping in July forced to stay in a small room with 250 pre-schoolers, as they sing 99 choruses of Jingle Bells, while banging their spoons against their water glasses.

As for the rest of you, may you have a joyous, last minute Christmas.

Chapter 3 - Holidays

'Slab Christmas Gifts' – December 21, 2006

I called up my friend Slab Marble a few days ago and wished him a Merry Christmas. Slab said he was glad to hear me say Merry Christmas instead of Happy Holiday since he was kind of an old-fashioned guy.

I said I took that to mean he didn't go around telling people to have a Happy Holiday and he replied I was wrong, saying while he didn't use the expression at Christmas, every Groundhog Day he made a point of telling people to have a Happy Holiday.

I decided to change the subject, and asked him if he had done all of his Christmas shopping. He said yes, and at a great sacrifice to his body. He told me that the parking lot at the shopping center was jammed and he had to park so far from the store, by the time he completed the long walk he had shin splints.

I told him that I certainly hoped he had learned his lesson on buying gifts for his wife and that he wouldn't do something dumb like the time he bought her a snow shovel for her birthday.

Slab said it was a much better shovel than the one she had been using and he couldn't understand why she hadn't realized his buying her a labor saving device was a thoughtful gesture. He also said he felt she overreacted by making him sleep out in the garage with the dog for a week.

Slab said be that as it may, for Christmas he had gone all out and not only bought his wife a new hedge trimmer, but knowing she had always wanted to travel, had splurged and was going to take her on a moose-hunting trip to Alaska. I said I not only wasn't sure about the hedge trimmer, but also had some serious doubts about how the moose-hunting trip would be received, since his wife doesn't hunt.

Slab accused me of being negative, and said that he was totally convinced his wife would be all choked up when she realized what he had given to her.

I said I didn't know about being choked up, but it wouldn't surprise me to learn that on Christmas morning, she became rather emotional, and for his sake and that of the dog, I just hoped he had a heated garage.

Chapter 3 - Holidays

'History of Halloween' – October 23, 2003

As many of you know, from time to time I alter my busy schedule and give a free history lesson. There is conclusive evidence that young people know very little about history, particularly when it comes to holidays.

Furthermore, polls have shown that Halloween, better known as 'Trick or Treat Day', the Fourth of July, better known as 'Set Fire to Half the County with Illegal Fireworks Day', and Christmas, better known as 'Santa Claus Day', are the only holidays young people seem to give a darn about.

There are thousands of kids who weren't even born the last time I gave my Halloween history lesson, so this is for them.

Halloween is a holiday that was created over fifty years ago by the Candy Manufacturers of America. At the end of each summer, the candy people were left with a mountain of leftover candy and no way to get rid of it. In an emergency meeting that was closed to the press one candy manufacturer from Chicago suggested that maybe they should invent a new holiday and call it Halloween.

A major component of the new holiday would be something called Trick or Treat. It would be patterned after a tried and true program that had proved to be very successful in Chicago for a number of years.

In the windy city, some guy named Bruno would stop by your place of business and say that if you would slip him some protection money, it would guarantee that nothing bad would happen to you or your store.

The candy manufacturer suggested a somewhat watered down version of this, called Trick or Treat. Kids would go door to door and shake down homeowners for free candy.

Initially the other candy people were skeptical, saying it was absurd to think that otherwise sane adults would actually be goofy enough to go out and spend huge sums of money on candy, and then turn around and give it away to little urchins, many of whom were total strangers.

However, everyone agreed that desperate times called for desperate measures so it was worth a try, even if the concept was admittedly ridiculous.

The rest is history. To the candy manufacturer's amazement, Halloween ended up being one of our major holidays, and the answer to the candy manufacturer's prayers. That concludes today's history lesson.

Chapter 3 - Holidays

'Columbus Day' – October 4, 2012

When I was a kid attending grade school in a small Montana town, Columbus Day was a pretty big deal. We didn't exchange gifts or get the day off from school or anything like that, but it was a pretty big deal nonetheless.

As I recall, we learned that Christopher Columbus got into a problem with authorities over the matter of selling the same piece of land to three different investors and was about to get tossed in the slammer. Fortunately, he had this thing going with the Queen of Spain and she pawned some jewelry and it enabled Chris to make the down payment on a ship called the Mayflower and leave town.

Someone had told him that if he kept sailing, he would eventually find a place where there was a lot of land, and he wouldn't be forced to sell the same chunk over and over to make a fast buck. Sure enough, he eventually discovered he was offshore in a place called Florida. It appeared that he had hit the jackpot and all he had to do was get off the ship, establish a land office and start raking in the money from investors.

However, the members of his crew looked around and discovered something on their own. They discovered this place was really out in the boondocks and there wasn't a Walmart store in sight and the place didn't even have a bar.

They threatened to water board Chris right there on the spot if he didn't turn the ship around and head back to Spain, which he was forced to do. But the fact remains he still had the satisfaction of knowing that he had discovered America.

I realize that at this point some of you might think I might be playing fast and loose with the facts and it is possible that my dissertation is not 100% historically correct, but in my defense it has been a long time since I was in grade school learning about Christopher Columbus and my memory bank has had quite a few withdrawals since then, but as the late Willard Fraser used to say, "History belongs to him what tells it."

Chapter 3 - Holidays

'Groundhog Day' – January 31, 2002

As I've noted in the past. I've always liked Groundhog Day and am disappointed that it is not a full-blown national holiday. I suppose the reason that it has never attained the status of a real industrial strength holiday where government workers get the day off, is that groundhogs don't have a lot of political clout. Groundhogs not only don't have deep pockets, they don't have pockets at all.

That probably explains why we don't exchange gifts, eat turkey, have a fireworks display, or do any of the things that would signify that Groundhog Day was a really big deal.

About the only thing that happens on Groundhog Day is that every news organization in the world sends reporters and camera people to some location that's about as remote as Lower Slobbovia, and they all stand around waiting for the groundhog to show up. It's usually a day that's even colder than the day the Olympic torch made its way across Montana.

In any event the groundhog, which had planned on sleeping until the middle of March, hears all of the commotion caused by the news people and pops its head out of the ground. It then sees Geraldo Rivera's shadow, which as we all know can be a very traumatic experience.

As soon as the groundhog sees Geraldo's shadow and all of the reporters and camera people, he immediately realizes that we will have six more weeks of news stories about Enron. Had the groundhog seen the shadow of someone from public broadcasting, the groundhog would have probably felt obligated to pledge some money.

Even though it has never become a big national holiday, it is obvious that Groundhog Day is a pretty big deal as far as the media is concerned, even though a lot of the members of the press tend to confuse it with the New Hampshire primary. This probably accounts for the fact that reporters covering the New Hampshire primary often mention the groundhog as being one of the early frontrunners for either the Democratic or Republican Presidential nomination.

Although in all fairness, in the last New Hampshire primary a groundhog could have held its own against at least half the candidates in the field.

Chapter 3 - Holidays

'New Year's Eve' - December 23, 1999

I realize it isn't even Christmas yet, but I am already thinking about the beginning of the New Year. Before you get all alarmed, I am not going to talk about the Y2K thing where some folks are predicting that the pop machines will go berserk and start spitting out Bud light, or when alligators will come out of storm sewers and start chasing dogs down the street. What I'm thinking about is the ghost of New Year's Eve.

I recall a time in my life when going out to one of the local watering holes and quenching my thirst on New Year's Eve was a really big deal. It's been quite some time since I did that.

Somewhere along the way, I realized that the usual predictable crowd at my favorite saloon had swollen to twice its normal size on New Year's Eve. Many of the new patrons were once a year drinkers and these folks were generally bad news.

There are always a certain percentage of them, who after getting half tuned up on two beers, would decide they were fighters or lovers or both. There were also those folks who, unaccustomed to drinking, would have a couple of glasses of Mogen David wine, get me cornered and tell me a lot more about themselves than I really wanted to know.

For some reason I didn't find it all that fascinating that the highlight of his particular individual's life had been being the president of his Victory Garden Club during World War II and that the local paper had done a story about the size of his parsnips.

Then at the stroke of midnight, I would find myself kissing some total strangers that I'd normally have second thoughts about even shaking hands with.

In all fairness, there were some parts of going to a local watering hole and living it up on New Year's Eve that were enjoyable. Occasionally, I even think it might be fun to do it again, proving once again that there's nothing more responsible for the good old days than a bad memory.

The thing that stops me is recalling what it was like waking up on New Year's Day, reviewing the event of the night before and thinking, "Oh, my God."

Chapter 3 - Holidays

'Snerd Christmas Letter' – December 16, 2004

The letter carrier who delivers our mail is a nice guy and does a good job come snow, rain, heat or gloom of night. There is only one time of year when I hate to see him coming up the driveway. In the days leading up to Christmas, I know that somewhere in his mail pouch will be the dreaded Snerd Family Christmas letter.

It is a well known fact that a number of people feel depressed during the holiday season and I am convinced that people like the Snerds are largely responsible.

It has been years since we've seen the Snerds but there is no statute of limitations when it comes to assaulting people with Christmas letters.

The letter usually goes something like this...

"Hello again!!! It's been another wonderful year for the Snerd family and we know you are anxious to hear about what's been going on in our lives. Following the election, Gaylord received phone calls almost every day from the White House urging him to be the next Secretary of State, but he declined, saying it would mean spending less time with his loving family. By the way, while Gaylord did treat himself to a new Rolls Royce after winning the $200-million Powerball Lottery, he has not forgotten the less fortunate and just yesterday dropped a dollar bill into a Salvation Army kettle.

Beulah, as you undoubtedly know, won the Pulitzer Prize for poetry and received a silver medallion for heroism for rescuing that family from a burning building.

Gaylord Jr. is president of the Honor Society and was named the most valuable player on the football team, the basketball team, and the baseball team.

Fido, our delightful poodle won sixteen blue ribbons at the National Dog Show."

Now if you're one of the people receiving the Snerd family Christmas letter and the highlight of your year was walking around for an hour trying to remember where you parked your car in the Walmart parking lot, you have every reason to feel depressed.

For the Snerds, I have this heartfelt holiday wish. May your upcoming year be filled with countless exciting events, beginning with having the horn on your new Rolls Royce get stuck while you are following a Hells Angels motorcycle gang down a deserted highway.

Chapter 3 - Holidays

'Thanksgiving' – November 21, 2002

A week from today, as all of you who have been paying attention already know, is a really big holiday. Yes, it's Thanksgiving, although it's understandable if a large number of people might be under the impression it's Christmas, since some of the stores have had their Christmas stuff on display for about six months.

I learned in school that Thanksgiving is the national holiday that commemorates the harvest of the Plymouth Colony. I'm reasonably certain it was the Plymouth Colony although it could have been the Honda Colony, but it happened a long time ago and there are no longer any eyewitnesses, so that part really isn't all that important.

The harvest followed a winter of great hardship when the water pipes froze, cars wouldn't start, the streets didn't get plowed and everyone blamed it on Miles Standish, the local weatherman.

When I say I learned all of this in school, I didn't actually learn it in the classroom. I learned it from my friend Cubby Skinner who was a little older than me. Cubby had an interesting sense of humor and recognized the fact I was somewhat gullible.

It wasn't until much later in life, when I was watching the History Channel that I learned that, on the first Thanksgiving, colonists and neighboring Native Americans sat down and shared a feast. At the time the Native Americans didn't have a clue that the colonists had these big plans to subdivide the entire country and sell it to wealthy outsiders.

I also learned that wild turkeys were served at the first Thanksgiving. As I recall, turkeys were the pilgrim's second choice, but were pressed into service at the last minute when the Pilgrims learned that crows were a protected species. This is something that all of us should be thankful for, since if it had gone the other way, we'd all be eating crow on Thanksgiving Day while watching ten zillion turkeys perch in our trees making a terrible racket and pooping on everything in sight.

Actually, the more I think about it, I can't say with absolute certainty that the thing about the crows is something I learned while watching the History Channel. It's possible it's something Cubby Skinner told me.

In any event, I hope you have a happy Thanksgiving.

'Turkey Growers' – November 25, 1999

I've always liked Thanksgiving because it is one of the real holidays, as opposed to one that a few creative folks at some government agency dreamed up so they could get the day off.

All of you who are students of history know that Thanksgiving is the day the Pilgrims set aside to give thanks for having survived both a Massachusetts winter, and a downturn in the economy, which they blamed on Alan Greenspan.

Even if the Pilgrims hadn't come up with the idea, we'd probably still have a November holiday, but perhaps with more commercial overtones. It may have come about when one day turkey growers discovered that they had ten zillion surplus turkeys and had to find a way to get rid of them. One turkey grower might have suggested creating an artificial holiday, designed to get people to buy turkeys.

Since the turkey growers wouldn't know much about manufacturing an artificial holiday, they would turn to the experts. Namely, the greeting cards people, the florists, and the federal government.

The turkey growers, being somewhat naive, might have suggested calling the new holiday "We're up To Our Necks in Turkey Droppings Day." The greeting cards people and the florists, who had agreed to help in exchange for a piece of the action, would have overruled them.

The greeting cards people would have claimed the turkey grower's proposed title was too long to fit on their cards. The florists who would have protested that "We're up To Our Necks in Turkey Droppings Day" was not something that would inspire a people to rush out and buy a dozen roses. Representatives of the federal government would say they didn't care what the new holiday was called, as long as they got the day off.

After a heated debate, almost as intense as when the Montana Legislature debated the issue of an open season on mourning doves, a compromise would be reached. All sides would probably have agreed to call the new holiday Thanksgiving, in honor of Fred Thanksgiving, the turkey grower who came up with the idea of creating another artificial holiday. On the other hand, maybe they'd have just called the new holiday, Fred.

Happy Thanksgiving.

Chapter 3 - Holidays

'Black and Blue Friday' – December 5, 2013

I saw my friend Slab Marble the other day and he was walking with a limp. I asked if his old war wound was acting up, the one where he snagged his backside on a nail while crawling under the army barracks to get out of KP duty.

Slab said actually he was a casualty of Black and Blue Friday. He reminded me that the Friday after Thanksgiving is the busiest day of the year for stores, with the exception of the day after Christmas when people are returning god awful Christmas gifts.

He said that he had decided to go to one of those big box stores in hopes of getting a smoking deal on whatever beer was on sale that week and didn't realize it was Black and Blue Friday. Slab said the store was jammed with people walking around with the same looks on their faces as seen on the faces of people on the television program "The Walking Dead."

Anyway, word got out that they were practically giving away smart phones at the other end of the store and a stampede started. He said he got knocked down, then stepped on by a little old lady who accused him of slowing her down and said if all of the smart phones were gone before she got there she would return and punch his lights out.

Slab said he decided to get out of there before she came back. When he limped out of the store, the parking lot was jammed, and he decided to sit in his '64 Cadillac for a few minutes recovering from his traumatic experience. He said his luck finally changed when a guy stopped and said, if he'd move he'd give him five bucks for his parking space. I told him you have to take your victories where you can get them.

Chapter 3 - Holidays

'Fruitcakes' – December 13, 2007

A while back, l was rummaging through some stuff and came across a hockey puck. This wasn't a hockey puck from my old hockey playing days since I didn't have any old hockey playing days. This was a CBS hockey puck. A number of years ago, someone at CBS came up with the brilliant idea of having the network carry hockey games. They sent out some hockey pucks in an effort to get the affiliates all excited about carrying the games. Unfortunately, the network discovered that hockey on TV was about as popular as hot dogs at a vegetarian convention.

Anyway, I still have the hockey puck, and every time I see it, I am reminded of fruitcakes, since some folks maintain they are both part of the same food chain and are about equal on the edibility scale.

With the holiday season upon us, I thought I would once again act as an early warning system, just in case you should be the recipient of a fruitcake. First of all, we should establish right off the bat, that someone who gives you a fruitcake does not necessarily have your best interests at heart. In all fairness, there are those who are thrilled to receive a fruitcake and if you have the digestive system of a shark and your favorite in-between meals snack is a hockey puck, I can understand why you might be thrilled.

However, there are also those who are not fruitcake lovers, and after receiving one, are looking for a way to dispose of it. I would caution you not to try to jam it down the garbage disposal. A friend of mine did this and there was a terrible clattering sound as chunks of metal flew all over the place. Then when he retrieved the fruitcake from the ruins, it wasn't even dented.

None of this is to say that fruitcakes don't have their uses. They can be invaluable if you have to scare off an intruder. The would-be burglar, who sees you standing there with a fruitcake in your hand, will assume you are offering it to them, which will prompt them to turn and run for their lives.

Some historians claim that a 10-pound fruitcake was the favorite weapon of Attila the Hun. Given his reputation for savagery, it's probably true.

Chapter 3 - Holidays

'St. Patrick's Day Swim' - April 26, 2001

I was taking a stroll in downtown Billings the other day and ran into my friend, Slab Marble. He asked me what was new, and I told him that I had been surprised to learn that a Montana Tech graduate student had discovered a living creature swimming around in the highly toxic waters of the Berkeley Pit in Butte.

Slab said he wasn't surprised and that he was pretty sure he knew what had happened. Given the intensity of St. Patrick Day celebrations in the Mining City, after consuming a gallon of green beer some guy told his buddies he was going to go skinny-dipping in the Berkeley Pit. He said the guy probably staggered over there, jumped in, and has been dog paddling around in the water ever since.

I told Slab he had it all wrong because all the media reports said the creature discovered swimming around had been identified as a water boatmen, an insect that can sing, in addition to fly, swim underwater and bite. Slab said leave it to the media to get the facts all messed up. He told me he was sure what they discovered paddling around wasn't a bug called the water boatman, it was a guy named Wally Boatman. He said Wally was a friend of his, and once when they were in Butte putting away a few cool ones, Wally claimed he could fly. Slab said Wally then jumped off the roof of the M&M, flapping his arms like crazy and ended up with two broken legs.

He said after Wally healed up, he then claimed he could swim underwater, even though he couldn't swim a lick. Slab said after his companions fished him out of the contaminated waters of Silver Bow creek, there was a big fight to determine the unlucky guy who would have to give Wally mouth-to-mouth resuscitation.

I conceded the fly and swim underwater part could lead some to suspect it was Wally, but what about the claim the critter could also sing and bite? Slab said Wally almost bit a guy's ear off long before Mike Tyson ever thought of it, and if the thing they discovered was singing "99 bottles of beer on the wall" there was no doubt in his mind that it was good old Wally.

I told him that as usual, it had been a thought provoking conversation.

Chapter 3 - Holidays

'White Sulphur Springs 4th of July' – July 4, 2003

When I was a kid growing up in White Sulphur Springs, the Fourth of July was a holiday we looked forward to almost as much as Christmas and the opening day of the big game hunting season.

These days, just before the fourth fireworks stands pop up like dandelions, but during World War II, fireworks were about as scarce as Republicans in Butte. However, that doesn't mean we weren't able to obtain some. All we had to do was con some adult into driving us to Helena.

These fireworks operations were undoubtedly illegal, and we were probably guilty of a crime, but by now the statute of limitations has run out. The place that sold fireworks was on the upper end of Last Chance Gulch, an area that also housed enterprises run by entrepreneurs like Ida, who rented rooms by the hour, and the Blue Moon operated by wrestler/saloonkeeper King Kong Clayton.

Helena later came down with a case of rampant urban renewal and these historic places disappeared, replaced by a multitude of little shops with ferns and no smoking signs.

But getting back to our fireworks shopping spree, the place where we made our purchases was the back room of a little store run by some Chinese. They seemed like really nice people but in all honesty, it wouldn't have mattered to us if it was run by the Chinese mafia as long as they agreed to sell us some fireworks.

Our top priority was stuff that made a lot of noise. The big red blockbusters were good, but the item we all wanted were things that were about two inches long and almost an inch across with a fuse in the middle.

These hummers could blow a two pound coffee can to smithereens. They are illegal in this day and age, and even the mention of them has been known to cause members of consumer protection groups to have a cow.

In looking back, the fireworks we used were downright dangerous, but we didn't need the government warning us that we'd be hurtin' cowpokes if one of these went off in our hand. We'd seen what happened to the coffee can, and there was no way we were going to risk doing anything that could cause damage to a trigger finger with the big game hunting season just 104 days away.

Chapter 4
GRAB BAG

"Slab said he bought the medicine to cure what was ailing him but some of the possible side effects were worse than what was ailing him so he tossed the medicine in the garbage can, had a cold beer, and immediately started to get better."

- Vic Miller

Chapter 4 - Grab Bag

'Lawrence Welk' – April 8, 2010

I was under the impression Lawrence Welk died in 1992, but Lawrence is proof that old orchestra leaders never die, they just move over to public television, where I spotted him last week.

For a number of years, our television station carried the Lawrence Welk show and Lawrence brought his orchestra to Billings on two separate occasions for performances at Metra.

Lawrence Walk was a really nice person. I don't mean to imply that we were close friends. We never played a round of golf together, although we did talk about golf one time. His manager was a guy who looked like Casey Stengel and Lawrence said he admired the way he could put backspin on a golf ball.

On the two occasions when the Welk show came to Metra, our station conducted a "Miss Champagne Music" contest. A number of young women entered the contest and we selected one as the winner. If the young woman were talented enough, she would be allowed to sing a song with the Welk orchestra.

For the initial Welk appearance, the young woman we selected met with Lawrence and he determined that she could sing with the orchestra. The second time we picked a young woman from Wyoming. Again, Lawrence wanted to hear her sing before determining if she could perform with the orchestra. If not, she would still be allowed to appear on stage and Lawrence would introduce her as "Miss Champagne Music."

The Welk people arrived in Billings the same day of the performance so we were a little crowded for time. Therefore, I picked up our "Miss Champagne Music" winner and we met Lawrence and his manager at the airport and we all drove from the airport down to the Northern Hotel. I was in the front seat with his manager and Lawrence was in the back seat with the young woman. He had her sing a song for him, was satisfied with the audition, and said he looked forward to having her perform with the orchestra.

She performed well that night, which was no surprise. The surprise came part way through the show when Tom Netherton, the orchestra's lead singer came down into the audience and sang a song to my wife, JoAnne.

I enjoyed knowing Lawrence Welk, and it is nice that he continues to live on, at least on public television.

Chapter 4 - Grab Bag

'Cloning Dolly the Sheep' - March 6, 1997

I had another call from my friend Slab Marble, and he said the cloning thing had him all excited.

I said he must have heard that earlier this week as I was getting into the elevator and all of a sudden, the doors slammed shut, and I almost got cloned the hard way.

Slab interrupted to say he wasn't talking about me, he was talking about Dolly. He then went on to explain that scientists in Scotland had cloned a sheep and that it was the spitting image of it's mother, and they named it Dolly.

I told Slab I didn't recall hearing about it, but conceded that I hadn't been tracking all that well ever since I got my bell rung by the elevator doors.

I did point out that I didn't see what the big deal was, since all sheep look alike anyway, so what was the point in cloning one?

Sounding somewhat disgusted, Slab said that if I'd actually showed up for my science class at White Sulphur High, instead of skipping out to go gopher hunting, I'd realize the significance of all of this.

He claimed it could have a great impact on medicine, agriculture and even theology. I said that by theology, I hoped he wasn't implying that someone had plans to clone Jim and Tammy Faye Bakker. He said he was quite sure that there was a specific law prohibiting anyone from cloning Jim or Tammy Faye.

Slab then went on to say that a Republican congressman was very upset about Dolly and had used words such as unethical and morally reprehensible. I pointed out that Dolly could probably use the same words in describing some congress persons.

Slab said that I could pooh pooh cloning all I wanted, but that he was looking forward to being cloned, saying it would able him to spend his days playing golf, while his clone worked and earned money.

I pointed out to Slab that I'd golfed with him and as I remembered it, he'd spent most of his time on the course yelling "fore" and apologizing to the people he hit. Therefore, I advised him that the world might be a safer place if he continued to work, and he let his clone play golf.

Slab promptly hung up on me. It was obvious he was beside himself, and a more pathetic couple you never saw in your life.

Chapter 4 - Grab Bag

'Goat Chops' – April 8, 1999

The other day I looked out the window and spotted some billowing clouds of smoke. I hadn't seen this much smoke since the fires in Yellowstone Park back in 1988 when the Park Service decided they wouldn't put out the little fires and then discovered they weren't able to put out the big ones.

I then realized the smoke was coming from the area of town where my friend Slab Marble lives, so I decided to get in the car and drive over to see if Slab was alright. When I got to his place it turned out that the smoke was coming from his back yard. Slab had fired up his charcoal grill to kick off the 1999 outdoor cookout season.

I asked him what the problem was and he said, "What problem?" He said charcoal grills always put off a little smoke the first time they're fired up. He then asked me what I was staring at. I told him he looked a little different, and to the best of my recollection, he used to have eyebrows.

Slab then admitted he might have been a bit generous with the lighter fluid, and when he lit the match the grill flared up a little bit.

As I was maneuvering around, trying to get out of the smoke, he said as long as I was there I might as well stay for dinner. I asked him if he was cooking some of that good Montana beef. Slab said that is what he normally had, but on this occasion he was having some grilled goat chops.

At this point I told him I was going to have to decline the dinner invitation since my doctor had recently told me to cut back on grilled goat chops.

The smoke lifted for a minute and when I looked at the grill, I mentioned that those were two of the biggest charcoal briquettes I'd ever seen, although they seemed to be burning nicely. Slab said those weren't briquettes, they were the goat chops and that he'd discovered that if you left them on the grill long enough, most of the flavor went away.

I told him that talking to him had been an educational experience, but it was time for me to leave. The fact of the matter is, I'd noticed six smokejumpers dropping out of a plane that had just flown over, and figured in about three minutes, Slab's back yard was going to get kind of crowded.

'Jackrabbits' – February 21, 2008

I had a call from my friend Slab Marble and he asked me if I had heard the news. I asked if he was referring to the news John McCain might pick Britney Spears to be his running mate. Slab said he wasn't talking about National Inquirer news, he was talking about real news, namely that Yellowstone Park had run out of jackrabbits.

I accused him of putting me on, but Slab swore he was telling the truth, and said scientists have concluded there aren't any jackrabbits in Yellowstone Park anymore and they don't know why. I told him I didn't know why either, but until they get to the bottom of it, it's a safe bet the anti-wolf people will blame it on wolves, and the anti-snowmobile people will blame it on snowmobiles.

He said that was probably true, but he's concerned that not having jackrabbits in the park will have a huge impact on park visitation, and visitors will stay away in droves. Slab said that when people think of Yellowstone Park, the two things they always think of are Old Faithful and jackrabbits. I told him I thought the two things were Old Faithful and buffalo, and when I was a kid, it was Old Faithful and freeloading bears.

Slab said he still missed the bears, but the mystery now is what had happened to all the jackrabbits. I told him as I recalled, after the freeloading bears became a nuisance, with cars stopping, causing big traffic jams, the bears mysteriously disappeared. The park people claimed they transplanted them. I asked if he knew of instances of tourists in Yellowstone stopping their cars, taking pictures of jackrabbits, and causing traffic to back up, which might have prompted the park people to transplant the jackrabbits. He said he might have read something about jackrabbit traffic jams in the National Inquirer.

Slab then said some of the same people who reintroduced wolves to Yellowstone, are considering reintroducing jackrabbits to the park, and asked how many I thought they should start with. I said knowing how prolific rabbits are, two should be enough. I told him that after reintroducing two young jackrabbits, the park would probably be overrun with rabbits in a couple of months.

Slab said he'd sleep better now, knowing that jackrabbits, the park symbol, will soon be back.

'Mourning Doves' – October 6, 2005

I had a call from my friend Slab Marble and he asked if I knew the dates of the mourning dove hunting season since he didn't want to miss it. I told him it was news to me that there was such a thing as a mourning dove season. I said in my younger days, I had hunted ducks and pheasants and while a couple of mourning doves hang out in our yard every summer and make a lot of mournful sounds, I've never looked upon that as being a shooting offense. Slab said some years back, Montana legislators in their infinite wisdom, decided to create a mourning dove season so guys like him would have something else to shoot at.

I asked if lawmakers had also created a hunting season on robins. Slab said as he recalled there was a proposal to create one, but he thought it got hung up in committee and never made it to the floor. I told him I'd observed a number of legislative sessions and that it is not uncommon for lawmakers to get involved in a lot of stuff such as nude dancing so important things like a robin hunting season often got lost in the shuffle.

I told Slab, since I'd never hunted mourning doves, I didn't know what the weapon of choice was, but since the doves in our yard spend a lot of time perched on a branch looking at me, he probably hunts them with a BB gun. Slab said his friends would laugh him out of town if he ever showed up in his camouflage outfit packing a BB gun, and that stud muffin hunters like him always use 12-gauge shotguns.

I then inquired as to how many mourning doves he'd gunned down over the years. Slab admitted that while he'd gone through about fifty bucks worth of shotgun shells, up to this point he hasn't actually dropped one. I then asked him if in the unlikely event his aim got better and he managed to bag one, did he plan to forego the turkey and invite all of his friends over on Thanksgiving to dine on the mourning dove?

Slab said he might just do that, and there'd be a lot more mourning dove to go around now that he had crossed me off his invite list.

'Not a Kid Anymore' – May 18, 2000

I hadn't heard from my old friend Slab Marble for a while and I was starting to get concerned that his distemper might have flared up again, so I decided to give him a call to make sure he was alright.

Slab answered the phone and, when I asked him if everything was ok, he said no, everything wasn't ok and didn't I have anything better to do than calling him up, asking dumb questions. I told him that whatever else might be wrong with him, I was glad his cheerful disposition was still intact.

Slab then said he was depressed because he suddenly realized he wasn't a kid anymore. I told him that was quite perceptive on his part but, given the fact that for years he has grumbling that Detroit hadn't made a decent car since the Rambler, it is possible he is starting to get a little long in the tooth.

I asked him if he was depressed because the clerk hadn't asked him to verify his age when he got to the checkout stand clutching a six pack of whatever beer was on sale that week. Slab said it wasn't that. It was the fact that when he left the grocery store with his six-pack he forgot where he had parked his car. I said that didn't prove anything, reminding him that he has always had a weird memory, as witnessed by the fact he can remember a joke he heard 20 years ago about a rabbi, a priest, and a goat, but he can't remember his wife's birthday.

Slab said maybe I was right, but another thing that bothered him was that in reading the obits, when someone died in their 80's he now assumed it must have been an accident that took the life of that relatively young person. He said when he was a kid, if he heard that someone had died in their 40's he assumed it must have been of old age.

I told Slab I thought he should quit worrying, pointing out he wasn't really all that old and was in remarkably good shape for a guy who drank beer and whose idea of exercise was bending the empty beer can in half.

He said come to think of it, something happened just last week that probably indicated he was still a real stud muffin. He said he was at a cocktail party and a woman he'd known for a number of years said she still found him to be about as exciting as Al Gore.

I agreed that a compliment like that doesn't come along every day.

Chapter 4 - Grab Bag

'Rock Scam' – January 1, 2004

I had a call from my friend Slab Marble and he said he wanted me to know that he was going to be a millionaire with his new money making plan. I knew I'd probably live to regret it, but I asked him to tell me about the plan. Slab said he was going to have people send him some money, and in return they could have a rock named after themselves.

I told him I thought this was a dopey idea even by his standards and asked what made him think people would be dumb enough to send him money to have a rock named after them. Slab said it was obvious I was out of touch with where it's at. He said he was listening to the radio and some guy was telling the audience that if they would send him $54, plus shipping and handling, he would arrange to have a star named after them, and they'd get a piece of paper verifying that one of the stars in the galaxy is now named Gullible Gillogly, or whatever the persons name happened to be.

Slab said this caused his thinking mechanism to trigger and he suddenly remembered that he owned two acres of land in eastern Montana that he had purchased sight unseen. The seller told him that it was prime farmland but when he went to check on his new property it turned out to be nothing but a big rock field with no vegetation. Slab said he was bummed at the time, but you never know how things will work out, and this property is going to make him a millionaire.

He said he planned an advertising campaign where everyone who sends him 50 bucks can have a rock named after them and they'll receive a certificate with Fred Flintstone's picture on it, verifying the transaction. I asked what would happen if someone showed up demanding to see their rock? Slab said that wouldn't be a problem. He said he'd just take them to the rock field, pick out a rock and tell them that it's their rock.

I had to admit that if thousands of people would send in money to have a star named after them, far be it for me to claim hundreds of people wouldn't send him money to have a rock named after them. Slab said I was finally starting to get the picture.

'Running of the Bulls' – July 18, 2013

I saw my friend Slab Marble the other day and mentioned that a lot of people had been injured this year in the annual running of the bulls in Spain. Slab asked if that was the event where a lot of people think it would be a good idea to voluntarily be chased down a street by a bunch of bulls with attitudes, and I told him that it was.

Slab said the blame lies with Ernest Hemingway who wrote about it a long time ago and now a bunch of people with mashed potatoes for brains show up every year and try it. He then wondered if Ernest ever actually ran with the bulls and I told him that Ernest was probably smart enough to sit on a bar stool in Spain and write about it without ever actually participating.

Slab then said the fact of the matter is you don't have to spend a lot of cash traveling to Spain to have the experience running from a bull and that it had happened to him right here in Montana. He said he was fishing one day, walked around a bend, and there was a huge bull standing where he wanted to fish. He told me he took off his red windbreaker and waved it at the bull to scare it away, but for some unknown reason, it didn't have the desired effect and the bull decided to charge him.

Slab said he dropped his fishing pole and took off at a dead run with the bull in hot pursuit and he barely escaped by setting a new high jump record leaping over a barbed wire fence.

He said, in all likelihood, he'd have been famous if Ernest Hemingway had been there to write about it. I told him that Ernest was probably sitting on a bar stool in Spain at the time.

'Service Agreement' – December 7, 2006

I hadn't heard from my friend Slab Marble for a while so I decided to call him to see if he was still among us. When he answered the phone, I asked how things had been going.

Slab said things were good even though he had experienced a bit of frustration on a recent shopping excursion. He said he had decided to get his wife a new hedge trimmer for Christmas, and everything was fine until he got to the checkout place. He said he knew the price, so he pulled out his wallet and slapped the money down on the counter and mentioned he was buying it for his wife.

The clerk then said she assumed he would also like to purchase a service agreement on the hedge trimmer. Slab said he told her he'd never heard of a service agreement and asked why she would assume he wanted one. The clerk said if the product quit working, the service agreement guaranteed that he could get it replaced. Slab said he pointed out he hadn't even paid for the product yet and was the clerk implying the hedge trimmer might die a dreadful death even before it had been taken out of the box?

He said the clerk assured him it was a wonderful product, but since he had a wife, he probably also had had life insurance, and a service agreement should be looked upon as being similar to life insurance. Slab said he told the clerk whether he had life insurance wasn't any of her business but to the best of his recollection, when they got married his wife hadn't purchased a service agreement on him.

Slab said the clerk then got a little huffy and told him she just hoped that if something went wrong with the hedge trimmer, he wouldn't regret not purchasing the service agreement.

Slab said if something went wrong with the trimmer, he would just bring it back and ask for a replacement, and if they didn't comply, he would stand there shouting that the store had sold him a piece of junk.

I had to agree that having Slab Marble standing in your store shouting at the top of his lungs that he'd been cheated would probably guarantee a replacement faster than any service agreement that has ever been written.

Chapter 4 - Grab Bag

'Siberian Tigers' – January 27, 2000

I had a call from my friend Slab Marble the other day and he asked me if I'd heard the news out of Zoo Montana about TJ and Nadia, the Siberian tigers. I told him I did recall hearing something about how the zoo had received permission to breed the two animals.

Slab said he was counting the days until he could go out and see the cubs. I cautioned him there was no guarantee that this thing was going to come off, because there was some concern TJ might have some problems with the mating thing.

Slab said the initials TJ must stand for tired and jaded. He said his uncle had that problem but thanks to Viagra he is now a new man. I told him I didn't think that was the problem since TJ is only seven years old, an age when tigers in the wild are real stud muffins. I said the problem is that TJ has led a very sheltered life. And by sheltered, I meant he hasn't even watched that program with two insects mating that they keep showing over and over on public television.

Slab said in that case the Zoo Montana people had better find TJ some positive role models right away. He said maybe they could send TJ to Hollywood for a week and he could hang out with Burt Reynolds. I reminded Slab that Burt was starting to get a little long in the tooth, and these days Burt's idea of a big evening might be watching a rerun of the Lawrence Welk show while sipping a glass of warm milk.

Slab said I might be right, but he did have one idea that might help TJ get with the program. He pointed out that the last time he was out there, the zoo has some rabbits in the children's zoo area. He said even in his prime, Burt Reynolds couldn't hold a candle to a rabbit, and if TJ spent some time watching those bunnies, he'd be a swinging Siberian in no time.

I allowed that might work and Slab said he hoped so, otherwise by the time TJ gets his act together, Nadia might wise up and insist on a prenuptial agreement...one stating, if things don't work out, she gets the tiger house and 80% of the tiger food. After talking to Slab, I've decided to call the zoo and suggest TJ and Nadia forget about having cubs of their own and just adopt a couple.

Chapter 4 - Grab Bag

'Smoke' – August 17, 2000

I was downtown recently and ran into my old friend, Slab Marble. I asked him what was new, and Slab said he had inhaled twelve thousand dollars worth of smoke in the last three weeks. When I questioned how he could put a dollar value on it, he said he was an expert on these things. He said I might recall that he used to smoke cigarettes, and that I probably also recalled that the way he held his cigarette caused many people to think of him as the ultimate suburban sophisticate. I told him my recollection was, the way he held his cigarette caused many people to think he was going to set himself on fire, but as the late Willard Fraser was fond of saying, "History belongs to him what tells it."

Slab said he would not dignify that comment with an answer, but getting back to my original question, being a former smoker qualified him as an authority, and he calculated he'd have had to buy twelve thousand dollars' worth of cigarettes to inhale the same amount of smoke that he's inhaled from the grass and forest fires in Montana.

Slab then said he was going to sue the state of Montana for making him inhale all of that secondhand smoke. When I told him I thought it was a dopey idea, he pointed out that the tobacco companies had just paid a zillion dollars to a lot of people who said they were smoke damaged, claiming they never noticed the warning on cigarette packages stating using the product might be harmful, and cause them to do weird things such as chase cars and run for president on the Reform party ticket.

I said this might be true but voiced doubt he could find a lawyer to take the case. Slab said he had a call in to attorney Algonquin J. Calhoun, a self-proclaimed legal giant. I told him I was somewhat familiar with the Algonquin. I said he once defended me in a jaywalking case, and I almost ended up getting the death penalty.

Slab said it didn't matter if Algonquin's legal skills might be a bit suspect, because once the state learned he might sue, they would probably agree to settle out of court. He said he then planned to take the money, trade in his 1964 Cadillac with the fender missing, and buy something really classy, like a 1989 Yugo.

I wished him well with his lawsuit and he walked away whistling, "Smoke Gets in Your Eyes."

Chapter 4 - Grab Bag

'Standardized Stuff' – January 4, 2001

Right after the first of the year I called up my friend Slab Marble to see if he was still among the living. Slab has been known to overdo things, particularly on New Year's Eve. My fears were unfounded as he informed me that he had reformed, and now stays at home on New Year's Eve and sips a glass of warm milk while watching a rerun of the Lawrence Welk Show. He said watching the Champagne Music Makers was as close as he got to the bubbly stuff anymore.

Slab said he got tired of getting up on New Year's Day and watching the Rose Bowl parade in color, even though he didn't have a color television set. I agreed bloodshot eyes have caused more than one party animal to reassess his lifestyle.

Slab said while he made it through the holidays ok, he was in a funk because of credit card problems. I said I found it hard to believe a guy who sent out used Christmas cards would go on a spending spree and max out his credit cards.

Slab said that wasn't it. He said his credit card problem was that when he went to the gas station the instructions said to do one thing with his credit card, when he went to the drug store the instructions were different, and when he went to the money machine to get some cash, they had still another set of instructions. He said he never knew whether the little black strip on the card should be on the top or the bottom or the inside or the outside and if he slid it through at the wrong speed the electronic contraption got indignant.

He asked me why the people who make stuff in this country couldn't get together and agree to standardize things. He says every vehicle he ever owned had a different way to unlatch the hood, and half the cars have the gas cap on the right side of the vehicle and the other half on the left side, and now no two credit card contraptions operate the same.

Slab said if members of Congress would quit passing dopey laws that complicate our lives and pass one calling for standardizing stuff to uncomplicate our lives, we'd all be a lot better off. Much as I hated to do it, I was forced to admit he had a point.

'Warning Labels' - October 11, 2001

I was at the grocery store the other day and spotted my old friend, Slab Marble. He was standing at the checkout stand, clutching a six pack of whatever beer was on sale that week, and trying to talk the clerk into giving him a senior citizens discount.

It was a good try, but he struck out. I mentioned that I hadn't heard from him recently, and Slab said he was feeling puny for a while and hadn't been his usual outgoing self.

I asked him if he went to a doctor and Slab said that he decided he could save a couple of bucks by just getting some stuff and doctoring himself. He told me he went to the drug store and found some medicine off the shelf that seemed like it was potent enough to cure what ailed him.

Slab said the problem was, when he got home and got ready to take a slug of the stuff, he noticed the word, WARNING. He said there were about a thousand words printed on the bottle, and they all seemed to be warning him not to take the medicine.

He said he was warned against using the medicine if he had chicken pox. It also cautioned him that taking it could cause a ringing in the ears, or loss of hearing. Slab said he was also advised not to take the stuff if he was pregnant, since it could result in complications during delivery.

He said the warning went on to advise him that taking the medicine could result in numbness, drowsiness, and blurred vision. He said at this point he was getting blurred vision from reading all of the warnings, but in thinking back, he believed it also advised him the medicine could cause bizarre behavior, such as the uncontrollable urge to watch reruns of the Lawrence Welk show.

Slab said that adding insult to injury, the final warning was not to drink any alcohol while taking the stuff.

I asked him if the medicine helped him get over feeling puny, and Slab said he never took any of it. He said he bought the medicine to cure what was ailing him, but some of the possible side effects were worse than what was ailing him, so he tossed the medicine in the garbage can, had a cold beer, and immediately started to get better.

I said I guessed it proved once again that sometimes the old ways are the best ways.

Chapter 4 - Grab Bag

'Graduation Commencement' – May 11, 2000

I keep hearing how budgets are tight at many schools in our area, therefore many of these schools are probably hard pressed to find the money that is needed to attract a first-class commencement speaker. I realize that some people who are running for office are eager to give commencement talks and don't charge anything, but who wants to listen to them?

Therefore, as a public service, I have agreed to once again give a commencement talk that all area schools can video tape and play back at their commencement ceremonies. The nice thing about my commencement address is that in addition to being free, it is mercifully short. I will give you a countdown and you can begin taping. 5-4-3-2-1.

"It is a pleasure for me to be here with all of you graduates, family and friends of graduates, school people, and those of you who dozed off during last year's commencement address and are still here. It is a real honor for me to be standing here in this stifling gymnasium, watching all of you use your programs for fans, and attempting to make myself heard over that screaming baby out there who has lungs like the late Howard Cossell.

I would urge all of you graduating seniors to go forth and find yourself well paying jobs so you can pay large sums of money into social security so old geezers like me can continue to play golf. Some of you young cynics are probably convinced that you will be paying into a program that will be broke before you get to collect anything from it.

That is not necessarily true. There is always a chance that the generation following you may be even dumber than you and will willingly pay twice as much in social security taxes, so you too could end up getting a social security check.

Those of you who haven't dozed off yet might think it is presumptuous of an old geezer to give young people advice but there are two things that old geezers are really good at. One is driving around with our left turn signal blinking, and the other is handing out free advice.

I leave with this thought. If you want to live a long healthy life, never eat anything you can't identify on sight and never buy anything that is only partially assembled. The only reason it is partially assembled is that the people at the factory couldn't figure out how to put it together either.

And this concludes this year's commencement address."

You can turn off the tape machine now.

Chapter 5
OBSERVATIONAL

"I realize there is probably something in the constitution that could be construed as guaranteeing people the right to wear shorts. Some folks who know just enough about the constitution to be dangerous."

- Vic Miller

Chapter 5 - Observational

'Academy Awards' – March 1, 2007

There is an unconfirmed report that they held the Academy Awards ceremony recently although I will have to confess this is just hearsay, since I no longer watch the event. The thought of watching a lot of people I've never heard of who starred in movies I didn't see has about as much appeal as watching a couple guys on television attempting to catch a fish.

There was a time when I thought the Academy Awards thing was a big deal and did watch. However, back then my wife and I saw quite a few movies and were familiar with both the films that were nominated for an award and the actors and actresses who were in the running for an Oscar. Another thing the awards show had going for it was that Bob Hope was the host and Bob was one of the truly funny people of our time. Even then, I wasn't too happy with the length of the Academy Awards show since it generally ran longer than the Civil War.

In talking with people who still have a deep interest in these kinds of things, it is my understanding the primary purpose of having the Academy Awards is no longer to honor actors and motion pictures. The awards have been reduced to being merely the vehicle that gives actors most of us have never heard of, a chance to display clothes while standing around on something called the Red Carpet. Most of the women are wearing dresses that cost more than the gross national product of many third world countries but still manage to look like they were designed by someone who had a few too many beers.

If you're wondering who won the Oscar's, I'm not sure any were handed out this year. I think after all that strutting around on the Red Carpet, all the nominees were so tuckered out they decided to skip the ceremonies, headed home and went to bed.

I did the same thing.

Chapter 5 - Observational

'Alleged' – July 24, 2003

On the old television show "Dragnet", when Joe Friday and his partner were tracking down lawbreakers, Joe would say 'just the facts, ma'am." Well, as you may have noticed, things have changed, and now it would appear there are no longer facts, givens or even assumptions.

Back then there might be a news story stating that local law enforcement people are looking for a local man in connection with a break-in that occurred last night. According to police, a number of eyewitnesses saw a dark-haired six-foot man in his 20's break into a home and then run down the street clutching some stolen property. Those witnessing the crime say, when seen leaving the crime scene, the perpetrator was wearing Levi's and a white t-shirt, and several eyewitnesses to the crime say they are well acquainted with the culprit and were able to supply investigating officers with his name.

In this day and age, the story would be sanitized and sensitized, made more politically correct, and would probably be more like this.

Local law enforcement persons are investigating an alleged crime that took place last night. Alleged eyewitnesses say the alleged suspect allegedly broke into a home and then allegedly ran down the street with some allegedly stolen property. The alleged suspect is believed to be in his mid-20's and is allegedly about six feet tall with dark brown hair. He allegedly was wearing Levi's and a white t-shirt, although this allegation has not been confirmed since the alleged eyewitnesses were not close enough to the alleged suspect to read the label on his jeans, and the alleged Levi's could have been a different brand of jeans. The alleged white t-shirt could have been an off-white t-shirt or even pale yellow.

While a number of the alleged eyewitnesses allegedly got a good look at the alleged suspect and allegedly identified him to authorities, claiming they have known the alleged suspect for a number of years, this is not to say that the alleged suspect actually committed the alleged crime or even that the alleged crime even took place. We hope to have more on this alleged story as more alleged details become available.

And getting back to Joe Friday and the old Dragnet show, he probably should have been saying, "Just the alleged facts ma'am," but somehow it just wouldn't have been the same.

Chapter 5 - Observational

'Crankers' – August 31, 2000

The other day I happened to think about cranks. By cranks I don't mean those people who write letters to the editor containing a lot of incoherent thoughts and misspelled words, but rather the cranks that were on early automobiles.

These days you get in the car, put the key in the ignition, turn it, it activates the starter, and the car starts, unless it's the day after the warranty runs out and then it's anybody's guess what will happen when you turn the key.

But when I was a kid, there were still quite a few Ford Model T cars around and they did not have electric starters. In order to start this particular vehicle, it was necessary to turn a crank, which was located on the front of the car. After adjusting the spark, the driver got out and turned the crank, which started to fire up the engine.

Watching someone attempt to start a car was great entertainment for kids in the small Montana town where I lived. We referred to the guy turning the crank as the 'cranker'.

The cranker, who always made a big production out of the cranking process when there were people watching, would turn the crank with a great deal of gusto. Most of the time the engine refused to cooperate. With each turn of the crank, the cranker got crankier.

As often as not, when the engine finally decided to fire up, the crank would swing around and crack the cranker on the wrist, causing the cranker to hop up and down while holding his wrist, and uttering words that would result in us kids getting our mouths washed out with soap if we had used them.

Now, watching a grown man hopping up and down like a deranged cottontail usually caused all of the juvenile spectators in attendance to go into such fits of laughter that we almost wet our pants.

The injured cranker for some reason failed to see the humor of the whole thing and often threatened to do a variety of things to us, none of them particularly appealing.

However, we weren't too concerned, knowing that instead of chasing after us, the cranker would always opt to jump in the Model T before the engine died forcing him to start the painful process all over again.

In thinking back, probably the only people who mourned the demise of the crank was the town doctor, who made quite a bit of money treating injured wrists and the town kids who lost their primary source of entertainment.

Chapter 5 - Observational

'Expiration Date' - July 26, 1990

The other night I was sitting at home, watching the news, and having a beer (a time-honored Montana tradition that I try to keep alive.) If the news is filled with depressing stories, such as rumors they might let TV evangelist Jim Bakker out of jail early, I've been known to have two beers.

This was only two-thirds of a beer news night, and when it was over I noticed something on the beer can that read "Best flavor if consumed before date on can bottom". I experienced a moment of panic at the thought I might be drinking expired beer, so I tipped the can to check the date, and poured about a third of a can of beer onto my lap.

It turned out the expiration date was something like the year 2050. I've noticed that people who put expiration dates on their products always seem to come with a date that approximates infinity.

As I was getting ready to dispose of the now empty beer can, I noticed something else. It read, "Government Warning: Consumption of alcoholic beverages impairs your ability to drive a car or operate machinery, and may cause health problems."

Now, this is all well and good, but as usual the government failed to warn serious beer drinkers about real life-threatening stuff. Otherwise, there would be a warning stating, "Getting tuned on this beverage may cause you to think you're tough, witty, and God's gift to women. This can bring about a confrontation with someone's 250-pound boyfriend and may result in your expiring long before the date on the bottom of this beer can.

Chapter 5 - Observational

'Fainting Goats' – November 8, 1990

I was reading where two ladies in Plentywood have some fainting goats. It seems these animals repeatedly stop, stiffen their legs, and keel over in a dead faint. If the symptoms sound familiar it may be because a lot of us had the same reaction when we received our property tax notices a couple of weeks ago.

In any event, these folks in Plentywood have 31 Tennessee fainting goats and people from miles around are showing up to see them faint. Apparently, these goats are a bona fide breed that has been traced back to the 1880's. They almost became extinct because Tennessee sheepherders kept the goats with their sheep and when the coyotes would attack, the sheep would run away but the goats would faint and be eaten by the coyotes. I have never looked upon sheep as being intellectual giants, but obviously they are rocket scientists compared to fainting goats.

In all fairness to the goats, they apparently faint because they have this combination of regressive genes, and as a result, becoming startled, they pass out for a little while.

Each baby goat is worth about $650, which is a lot of money. I have the feeling that if you owned one of these and saw a coyote approaching your goat, it might be touch and go as to who fainted first, you or the goat.

I thought I'd tell you about all of this because with Christmas coming up you might want to buy one as a gift. However, if you think $650 might be a little too much to pay for a goat that faints, for $25 I think I might be able to get you a rabbit that will throw up on your rug.

Chapter 5 - Observational

'Legalized Gambling' – January 20, 2000

The matter of legalized gambling in Montana is sometimes a rather emotional issue. There are those who feel that there should not be any type of legalized gambling. Some of these folks oppose it for good reasons, while others simply oppose any vice they are not involved in at the moment and at the moment gambling is not one of their vices.

On the other end of the gambling teeter-totter we have folks with an insatiable appetite for gambling, are not satisfied with what we have now, and feel we need even more.

I grew up at a time when slot machines and punchboards were common sights in Montana and the fact that we have legalized gambling is not something that keeps me up nights. I buy an occasional lottery ticket, think we have too many casinos, am aware of the fact the revenue from gambling pays for a big chunk of running city government and while I wouldn't sign a petition to abolish gambling, I don't feel we need more.

For those people who feel the need to get into heavy duty big time gambling, I have a suggestion. Get into the ranching business. Las Vegas doesn't quote odds on the game of ranching but if they did, they'd probably give you 5-1 odds that, what little rain we get during the summer, will come during haying season, and 6-1 odds that a nearsighted hunter will mistake your prize bull for an elk and promptly gut shoot it. They would give you 7-1 odds that calving season and the most miserable weather of the year will occur at the same time, and 100-1 odds that the price of everything you have to sell will go down, while the price of everything you have to buy will go up.

If you get into the sheep business, the oddsmakers in Vegas would probably advise you that your lambs are 21-point underdogs to a pack of coyotes in the annual "Survival Bowl."

So if anyone out there isn't content with lottery games and poker and keno machines and would like to indulge in some additional legalized gambling, I suggest you buy yourself a ranch and deal yourself in. If you are the type who will bet the grocery money that you can fill an inside straight, you're going to love the ranching business.

Chapter 5 - Observational

'Mars' – April 8, 2004

Well, the government is up to its old tricks again and is trying to make us believe that they have actually landed something on Mars. You'll probably recall they did the same thing back in 1997 when I did my first expose of their trickery. At that time NASA claimed that a thing called the Sojourner was bumping along on the surface of Mars. The landscape was barren and lifeless and looked like the kind of property you'd probably end up with if you bought some land sight unseen on the internet from some guy named Buster. The Sojourner itself looked like your car would look if you left it in a very bad neighborhood for about fifteen minutes and the locals stripped it, taking everything of value.

Back then I did a commentary revealing it was all a hoax and this thing wasn't sending back pictures from Mars, it was sending back pictures from a remote location in eastern Montana. You may recall I predicted that if you kept watching the pictures being transmitted from what the government claimed was Mars, sooner or later an antelope would appear on the screen being chased by a bunch of guys in a pickup with Daniels County license plates. The government apparently got word I was wise to them so they shut down the operation before my claim could be verified.

The passage of time has obviously emboldened the government to try it again. This time instead of a stripped down car they are using a couple of things that look like two pieces of farm equipment. The government originally wanted to name them Click and Clack after the Tappet brothers to give the operation some credibility, but cooler heads prevailed. Once again authorities maintain these things are on the surface of Mars and even claim there are indications the place might have had some water at one time and could even have supported a primitive form of life. That last statement convinced me that while it is still a hoax, this time instead of eastern Montana, the pictures are being sent from a location in North Dakota.

Right now, I realize I'm a voice crying in the wilderness, but any day now those tabloids by the checkout counters at grocery stores will confirm everything I just told you and I'll be vindicated.

Chapter 5 - Observational

'Physical Checkup' – April 4, 2002

I recently went down to the Billings Clinic for my annual physical checkup. I suppose if you really want to get technical about it, it was actually my "I've been meaning to get down here for the last couple of years" physical checkup.

What prompted me to finally get around to it was that the gentleman who has been my doctor for the last 20 years is going to retire. I've only had two primary doctors since I came to Billings back when the crust of the earth was cooling. I've liked both of them and now it appears I'll have to adjust to a new doctor. I feel a little bit like a baseball player who's been with the same team for a long time and has just been told he's been traded.

The friendly nurse had me stand on the scale and recorded how tall I was and how much I weighed. I weighed about 165 pounds and measured 71 ½ inches with my shoes on. I mention this for the benefit of those people who watch me on television and are convinced I can't be more than five feet tall.

As part of the exam, I had to remove my clothes and put on one of those gowns with the opening in the back. I'm not very good at reaching back and tying the little cloth things that keep the gown closed. Although I guess it's one of those things you don't want to ever get good at.

I'm never too thrilled with the part where I have to have some blood drawn. However I was afraid if I made a big fuss, they'd put me in one of those restraining outfits like they made Hannibal Lecter wear in "Silence of the Lambs." Actually the people in the lab were all very nice, including the lady who drained all the blood out of my body. Contrary to what you may have heard, she does not have vampire teeth.

When all was said and done, the consensus was I still have a pulse, which I consider to be good news. I'm still a little upset about my doctor retiring, but I am not ready to concede that it is a done deal. I'm still holding out hope that like Michael Jordan, he'll sit out a season or two, change his mind, and announce he's going to unretire.

'Potbelly Pigs' - July 23, 1992

I've decided to throw caution to the winds and discuss one of the more pressing problems confronting Billings, and the nation. Namely, potbelly pigs. I realize this is an election year, but contrary to what you may be thinking, this is not going to be a "throw the rascals out" commentary.

This week, the Billings City Council voted 6-4 to prohibit pigs from living in Billings. This includes the miniature Vietnamese potbelly pigs that a number of people have apparently fallen in love with and claim they are the ultimate pet. These pigs often cost over $1,000 and are supposed to stop growing when they are about a foot tall and weigh about 50 pounds. Potbelly pigs are also supposed to have sweet dispositions. In spite of these admirable virtues, the Council ruled they cannot live in Billings. I don't know if that is the last word on the subject, or if the ACLU will file a suit claiming the Vietnamese potbelly pigs' constitutional rights have been violated.

However, even in enlightened communities where pigs can live wherever they want, and presumably even get married, all is not tranquil in the pig world. It seems some unscrupulous pig peddlers are palming off pigs billed as miniature, and the buyers are later discovering to their dismay that they are the owners of pigs that are growing faster than the national debt.

One woman in Pennsylvania bought what was supposed to be a miniature potbelly pig. Her pig now weighs 175 pounds and has the disposition of Don Rickles. It backed her husband into a corner, demanding a dog biscuit until he cried for help. At this point, most of us would have held a going away party for the pig but the woman says she will never give it up claiming it is now a member of the family.

At the risk of being judgmental, it would appear that in this case, the pig is not the only a member of the family, it is by far the smartest member of the family.

Chapter 5 - Observational

'Shorts' – June 19, 1997

Now that summer is more or less here, one sees more and more people out and about wearing shorts. This prompted several people to ask me if I planned to repeat a commentary I did on the subject about seven years ago.

Since this is a rather quiet week, I figured, why not?

According to the song, summertime is supposed to be the time when the "livin' is easy." While the song neglects to mention it, summertime is also the time when a lot of us take leave of our senses and decide that we would look good in shorts.

Actually, a small segment of the population actually does look good in shorts. As I recall, the last time they did a count, they discovered that 23 Americans looked good in shorts. Unfortunately, when the rest of us wander around in shorts, the overall look ranges from "barely tolerable," to "oh my god." People have been known to giggle themselves into life threatening comas as the result of seeing other people in shorts.

It is obvious that we need some kind of a law to regulate the wearing of shorts. I am of the opinion that there should be a seven day waiting period before anyone is allowed to buy a pair. This would allow adequate time for authorities to conduct a background check, and perhaps even a profile check. Officials could then determine if the person would pose a threat to society if allowed to buy shorts and wear them in public.

I realize there is probably something in the constitution that could be construed as guaranteeing people the right to wear shorts. Some folks who know just enough about the constitution to be dangerous, will probably claim that if we have the right to bear arms, we also have the right to bare legs and thighs.

While I certainly don't want to stomp on anyone's constitutional rights, I am concerned that if we don't get a law on the books soon, one of these days someone like Roseanne Barr or Raymond Burr will decide that they would look good in shorts, buy them, and wear them in public.

That, for all practical purposes, would signify the end of the civilized world as we know it.

Chapter 5 - Observational

'Street Crossing Buttons' – October 12, 2006

The other day I was standing on the curb waiting to cross a busy street and noticed the little button on the metal pole. Theoretically, by pushing the little button it would cause the traffic signal to change from the don't walk symbol to the walk symbol.

I didn't push the little button. The reason I didn't push the little button was I recalled a commentary I did back in 1989. After researching the matter, I had determined that if I pushed the little button, the signal would change from don't walk to walk in one minute. If I didn't push the little button, it would be a full sixty seconds before the signal changed from don't walk to walk. It was obvious to me the little buttons on the poles weren't connected to anything.

I figured what probably happened was the city was getting complaints from a few pedestrians who were mad because they had to wait to cross the street. In some instances, there might not have been a moving vehicle within a block of the intersection, but the signal indicated don't walk so they just stood there like statues.

Now the person at city hall listening to their complaints could have told them if they'd give the matter some thought, they'd realize that when they there isn't a vehicle within a block of them, most people simply ignore what the contraption with the walk and don't walk symbols indicate, and just cross the street.

However, people connected with government are always reluctant to tell people to start thinking because this could snowball and before you know it, people might even start thinking when they are in a voting booth, which could have serious consequences.

Therefore, to cut down on the complaining, the city came up with the idea of putting little buttons on metal poles. Pedestrians could push the buttons and by doing so, it helped pass the time of day while waiting for the signal to eventually chance. People would actually believe they were speeding up the process, even though the button wasn't connected to anything. Perception almost always triumphs over reality.

The next time we have a rating period, our television station will probably do a five-part expose on this, using hidden cameras and stuff. In the meantime, you'll just have to take my word for it.

Chapter 5 - Observational

'Laws' – July 20, 2000

A few days ago, I found myself standing behind Slab Marble in the checkout line at the grocery store. He was carrying a bottle of prune juice and was trying to convince the clerk she should give him a five-cent discount even though the coupon he presented had expired two years ago.

While the clerk was trying to get hold of the manager to ok this questionable transaction, Slab turned to me and said he'd read once that we had ten million laws on the books, attempting to enforce the Ten Commandments.

I asked him what prompted this Kung Fu flashback and he said it was probably a law that the Billings City Council passed to keep people from taking beer and whisky bottles to the park. He said in that case, why didn't they just pass a law saying that? I told him I didn't know, and he said he could envision a call on police radio telling officers to break off a pursuit of a bank robber and head for Pioneer Park because the Smith family had been seen entering the park with a picnic basket containing a small glass jar of mayonnaise.

I said I couldn't see that happening, and maybe the reason they included all glass containers instead of just beer and whisky bottles was that the council was concerned people walking around in their bare feet might cut themselves on a broken mayonnaise jar. Slab asked why the council didn't just pass a law saying no one would be allowed to walk around in his or her bare feet?

He reminded me that the city has some kind of a law making it illegal for minors to possess tobacco but there are kids smoking cigarettes all over the place. He said as far as he knew, we still have a law against jaywalking, but people jaywalk all the time. And he said the law saying people taking their dogs for a walk must clean up the mess when their canines poop on other people's lawns, is a real joke.

He said before any government body passes a law, they should meet first with the law enforcement people responsible for enforcing the law and if they say it's not enforceable, the proposed ordinance should be placed in the "Get Lost" file.

At this point the clerk agreed to give Slab a five-cent discount on his prune juice and our high level discussion about goofy laws came to a merciful end.

'8th Grade Education' – October 18, 2001

There was a time when a lot of folks only had an 8th grade education. When we hear this, a lot of us tend to think of these people as being barely literate. We may have been a bit hasty in our judgment.

Someone recently came across an 8th grade final exam given to students in Kansas back in 1895. Here are some of the things on the exam....

- Give nine rules for the use of capital letters.

- What are elementary sounds and how are they classified?

- Name the parts of speech and define those that have no modifications.

- Name and define the fundamental rules of arithmetic.

- District No. 33 has a valuation of $35,000. What is the necessary levy to operate the school seven months a year at $50 per month and have $104 for incidentals?

- Find the interest of $512.60 for 8 months and 18 days at 7%.

- Name all the republics of Europe and give the capital of each.

- Describe the process by which the water of the ocean returns to the sources of rivers.

- Describe the movements of the earth and give the inclination of the earth.

- What is the cost of 40 boards 12 inches wide and 16 feet long, at 20 cents per foot?

These were just some of the things that 8th grade students were expected to know in order to get their diploma.

It would be interesting to see how today's college graduates would do on that test.

'Dinosaur Roar' - August 9, 1990

I was going to talk about the proposed budget deficit reduction plan and how it's going to affect your lives, when it occurred to me that I don't have the foggiest idea how it's going to affect your lives.

I realize that a lot of our elected officials don't have the foggiest idea either, but that doesn't stop them from talking about it. But I've never looked upon them as the world's greatest role models, so I have decided to talk about dinosaurs.

Dinosaurs are a big deal in Montana these days. People with beards keep digging up dinosaur bones and there is a renewed interest in these critters, including the mystery of what caused them all to die. Contrary to what your mother may have told you, it wasn't because they refused to eat their cooked carrots.

In any event, they have recreated a dinosaur at the Museum of the Rockies in Bozeman, and it makes this awesome roaring sound, which reminded me of the sound my second grade teacher made when she caught me erasing the eyeballs out of George Washington's portrait in my history book.

While the roaring sound was impressive, my keen mind (honed to a fine edge by years of investigative reporting and a number of cold six packs) caused me to ask myself, "how do we know that's an authentic sound"?

We will probably never know, since I think the only people who were around when these creatures roamed the earth are three members of the U.S. Supreme Court, and no one wants to wake them up and ask them about dinosaurs for fear they will make some idiotic rulings that will complicate our lives.

So, when you stop by the Museum of the Rockies, just enjoy the dinosaur, and don't worry about the authenticity of the sound.

Chapter 6
POLITICS & TAXES

"I know that most of you were as shocked as I was when, on election night, Dan Rather announced that the network had declared a winner in the presidential race, and it wasn't me."

- Vic Miller

'Legislative Quiz' – January 2, 2003

Every two years we have a session of the Montana Legislature. The lawmakers convene on odd years as opposed to even years which quite possibly could account for the fact we often have rather odd legislative sessions. On the other hand, it could have something to do with a full moon. However, I'm not here to speculate on why lawmakers act goofy. I am here to conduct a short quiz to find out how much you know about the Montana Legislature.

To cut down the odds of your ending up feeling like an ignorant clod, we are going to make this multiple choice, so even if you are an ignorant clod, there's always a chance you'll get lucky. In addition, since we don't want to take up too much of your time, we are only going to have you answer three questions.

Question number one. In order to be a legislator, you must be able to prove you have one of the following:

a. A college education.

b. A high school education.

c. A pulse.

Question number two. When lawmakers talk about revenue enhancement it means:

a. Putting furniture polish on the revenue and buffing it to make it look better.

b. Lawmakers plan to contribute their own salaries to the general fund.

c. While we're all distracted trying to figure out what in the heck revenue enhancement means, lawmakers will be raising our taxes.

And Question number three. Lawmakers will solve the really big budget deficit by:

a. Staying in session until April 20 and hoping for the Easter Bunny to bail us out.

b. Standing on street corners asking passersby if they have any loose change.

c. Hiring the Arthur Anderson accounting firm to show the deficit is actually a surplus.

Actually, I don't have time to figure out how many questions you got right, so in scoring just give yourself one point for every question you answered, and no points for every question you didn't answer.

If you answered at least one question, you have earned the right to be called a knowledgeable taxpayer. On the other hand, if you didn't answer any of the questions it's obvious that you are a befuddled taxpayer. In any event you've all have earned the right to pay lots of taxes and frankly I don't know what the state would do without you. Congratulations.

Chapter 6 - Politics & Taxes

'My Election Loss' - November 7, 1996

I know that most of you were as shocked as I was when on election night Dan Rather announced that the network had declared a winner in the presidential race, and it wasn't me.

Let's get real here. There is no way I could have lost. Everyone I talked to said they planned to vote for me. Furthermore, I ran the kind of campaign people claim they want to see. I did not receive any illegal campaign contributions, or very many legal ones for that matter. I declined to put up unsightly yard signs and refused to attack any of the other presidential candidates, even the ones who were obvious meatheads.

In spite of all this, the networks claimed that Bill Clinton won the race. However, I have refused to concede, since there is no doubt in my mind that I won. This is obviously just another effort on the part of the current power structure to maintain the status quo and steal the election. For example, I can't get anyone to tell me how many votes I got.

Since they refuse to tell me, it's obvious that they have something to hide. According to the information I have been able to obtain, there are about 196-million eligible voters in this country. Now let's look at the vote totals that we have been given by the people in charge. They claim that Bill Clinton, Bob Dole, Ross Perot and all of the lesser candidates wound up getting a combined total of about 96-million votes. Subtract this from the 196-million and that leaves about 100-million votes that are unaccounted for. So, what happened to these votes?

The people who comprise the current power structure would have us believe that these people never showed up at the polls, but we all know better. It's obvious that all of these people showed up and voted for me, and there is this giant conspiracy to deny me the presidency. I'm not sure where all the missing ballots are, but the first place I would look would be the basement of the white house.

At this point I am not sure what my next step will be since my attorney, Algonquin J. Calhoun, still hasn't been able to get his license back after being disbarred, but trust me, we plan to do something about this miscarriage of justice.

'President's Visit to Billings' – November 9, 2000

At the time I wrote this commentary, we were still waiting for the people of Florida to determine the next president of the United States. At the time I wrote this commentary the people of New Hampshire were running around making squeaky sounds claiming this must be illegal since it is the people of New Hampshire, not the people of Florida who have always determined who the next president of the United States will be. They do this by holding the New Hampshire primary election very early in the year, before the rest of us have even finished singing "Auld Lang Syne."

While I may not know who the next president will be, as a wildly recognized historian I can tell you that sooner or later, when he runs out of other places to visit, the next president of the United States will visit Billings.

I know this because every president of the United States, after running out of other places to go, visited Billings. All of us widely recognized historians know that, when George Washington visited Billings, he attempted to skip a Susan B Anthony dollar across the Yellowstone River. I am aware that some historians claim that it was Susan B Anthony and not a dollar that he attempted to skip across the Yellowstone, but these are second-rate historians and don't know what they are talking about.

As you may or may not know, Abraham Lincoln visited Billings, walking all the way from Washington, D.C. to return a book he had borrowed from the Parmly Billings Library. The book was quite a bit overdue and Honest Abe had to split about twelve thousand logs to raise the money to pay the fine.

Ronald Reagan visited Billings and rode around Metra on a stagecoach before stopping to chop what he thought was some brush, but turned out to be the Christmas trees on display at Metra for the annual Festival of Trees.

George Bush Sr. paid us a visit during the Big Sky State Games and finished third in the sack race. He attributed his poor showing to jet lag. Finally, Bill Clinton came to town, stopped at the Kit Cat Café, wolfed down ten burgers and designated the place a National Monument.

So, while we may not know who the next president of the United States will be, what we do know is that sooner or later he will visit Billings. I for one am really looking forward to it.

'Politically Correct' – August 3, 2009

I saw my friend Slab Marble the other day and asked him what he'd been up to. Slab said he'd been back to his hometown and had been accused of being politically incorrect. I asked what brought that about. He said he was in one of the local watering holes having a cool one and asked the guy on the bar stool next to him if the dismal swamp on the edge of town was still there.

Slab said the guy got all huffy and said there was no such thing as a dismal swamp and if he was referring to the wonderful wetland area on the edge of town, it was doing very nicely. He then accused Slab of being politically incorrect and said it would be appreciated if he refrained from referring to the area as a swamp. Apparently, people will write out a check to save a wetland, but they are somewhat reluctant to write out a check to save a swamp.

Slab said up until then he hadn't realized he was a politically incorrect person, but it appears he's been using a lot of politically incorrect words.

He said he learned that you no longer refer to someone as an alcoholic. They are now anti-sobriety activists. If someone undergoes a sex change, it should be referred to as having a gender re-assignment. And no one is clumsy. They are uniquely coordinated.

I told him I found all of this quite enlightening and asked him if he had any more examples of words one should avoid using.

Slab said I should avoid calling those people who sneak over the border illegal aliens, since that would probably hurt their feelings. Instead, they are undocumented immigrants. And those people at street corners with cardboard signs are not panhandlers. They are applicants for private sector funding.

Furthermore, garbage men are now sanitation engineers and janitors are custodial artists. I had to admit I didn't know that and now when I'm taking out the garbage and sweeping out the garage it will make me feel a lot more important.

As we parted, I thanked him for the lesson in political correctness, and in the future, I would try not to use politically incorrect words since I didn't want to appear to be stupid. Slab said no one is stupid anymore, the correct term is intellectually impaired.

'Clinton Wedding' – August 5, 2010

I had a call from my friend Slab Marble and he said he was all bummed out because it had happened again. I asked what he meant, and he reminded me that back in 2005 when Prince Charles got married for the second time, some incompetent at the palace obviously put the wrong zip code on the envelope and he never received his invitation to the wedding.

I said I did have a vague recollection of that happening. Slab said once again he's been the victim of a mix-up. He speculated that Hillary must have had a lot on her mind when she was addressing all of the invitations and obviously send his to Afghanistan instead of Billings so he didn't get the invitation to Chelsea's wedding.

I said I hated to be the one to tell him but there was an outside chance that he hadn't been invited to either one of these events. Slab conceded there was a remote possibility he hadn't been invited to Charles wedding since he had written a letter to the editor once saying Queen Elizabeth always looked like she was on her way to participate in a goofy hat contest.

However, he said as a major campaign contributor to Bill Clinton's last presidential campaign he fully expected to be invited to Chelsea's wedding. I asked the amount of his major contribution and Slab said he'd mailed five bucks to Bill's campaign headquarters. I pointed out that some might not consider that a major contribution and Slab said it was about what he usually pays for a six pack of whatever beer is on sale, so as far as he is concerned it was a major contribution.

He said he'd even purchased a wedding gift for the happy couple. It was a really nice frying pan, and not only that, he had gone to the expense of having his suit cleaned in anticipation of going to the wedding. I asked if that was the suit that looked exactly like the one that Barney Fife used to wear when he got dressed up on the Andy Griffith show and Slab said that was the one.

I told him that it really was unfortunate that he hadn't been able to attend Chelsea's wedding since with a classy suit like that, he would have fitted right in.

'Governor Marble' – July 10, 2003

I saw my old friend Slab Marble jaywalking across the street the other day and told him he should be ashamed of himself and that jaywalking was illegal and he could get arrested. Slab said about as many people get arrested for jaywalking as get arrested for shooting fireworks inside city limits.

I admitted he had a point and then asked if he was still planning on running for president as we had discussed right after the first of the year. Slab said he watched the Democratic candidate's debate and realized he was overqualified, so he'd decided to run for governor instead.

I told him I did recall that he had a full head of steam built up to run for governor in 2002 until I pointed out he was two years early. Slab said that had been a rather traumatic experience but that he had managed to keep a stiff upper lip and was ready to have another go at it. I asked him if he was going to run as a Republican or a Democrat and he said he hadn't decided, since both parties appear to have platforms built with planks that are a little warped.

I inquired as to what he planned to do if he were elected. Slab said the first thing he would do would be to commute the sentences of the highway patrolmen who have been guarding the governor. He said the patrolmen should be out on the highways improving Montana's cash flow by arresting speeding drivers from New Jersey. Slab said he wouldn't need bodyguards since he'd just have his wife follow him around and if anyone got out of line, she'd frown at them. He said that's all it's ever taken to get him to shape up.

I noted that people keep saying we need higher paying jobs and asked if he had a plan to solve this. Slab told me he was a firm believer in higher paying jobs and that's why he was running for governor. He said the job pays a heck of a lot more than his present job.

He then admitted he didn't have a campaign slogan and asked if he could borrow the one I used when I ran for president, which was "No goofier than the rest of them."

I told him to be my guest.

Chapter 6 - Politics & Taxes

'Montana Lullaby' – February 22, 2007

I had a call from my friend Slab Marble and he asked me if I was aware of what the Montana Legislature was up to. I told him I try to avoid keeping track of what the legislature is up to since I find it to be too depressing.

Slab said legislators were considering passing a law to create something called an official Montana lullaby. I asked Slab how many cans of beer he had consumed before calling me.

Slab swore he hadn't had a drop, but he wasn't sure about some of the lawmakers in Helena. He said it looks like we're going to have an official state lullaby, unless Montana Governor Swartzneiger vetoes the measure. I pointed out that Montana's governor was Brian Schweitzer, and Arnold Swartzneiger was California's governor. Slab asked if Brian was the one with the funny accent or the one who wears the shoestring around his neck. I said Arnold's the one with the accent, and that isn't a shoestring around Brian's neck, it's a bolo tie.

He then asked if I knew what in the heck a lullaby was. I told him according to the dictionary, it was a song for lulling a baby to sleep. Slab said there's no need for an official state lullaby and if somebody has a baby that needs lulling, they should just take the kid to Helena and expose it to a legislative debate. He said those debates have been known to cure chronic cases of insomnia when all else has failed.

I asked Slab if his mother ever sang a lullaby to him when he was a baby. Slab said his mother wasn't into lulling, but she'd put a couple of records on the record player and pretty soon he'd be out like a light. He said his favorites were Homer and Jethro singing, "When it's Tooth Pickin' Time in False Teeth Valley," and "Roll On Deodorant, Roll On."

I said his mother probably wasn't aware that exposing him to that kind of music at such an early age could have caused permanent brain damage. Slab said that's been known to happen, and if lawmakers go along with the official state lullaby thing and then take a lot of heat when they go back home, their defense might be they were under the influence of Homer and Jethro at the time.

'Parliamentary Government' – March 8, 2001

I saw my friend Slab Marble recently and he said he'd heard that the Montana Legislature was giving some thought to televising legislative sessions. I told him some lawmakers had talked about it, saying it would be a public service. Slab said he felt that was kind of a stretch, unless curing chronic cases of insomnia is their idea of a public service.

He then asked me if knew Bob Kelleher. I told him that I knew Bob well and had felt his pain when he was an unsuccessful candidate for Congress, Governor, and President of the United States. I pointed out he did get elected and was a delegate at Montana's 1972 Constitutional Convention, but I never held that against him.

Slab said the best idea that Bob ever had was to change our system to a Parliamentary form of government, and if Montana did that, he would watch televised sessions of the legislature.

He said he was channel surfing one night. On one of the channels he came across, what he thought was one of those wild skits on Saturday Night Live. However, it turned out to be British Prime Minister Tony Blair, who was down on the floor of Parliament trying to explain stuff, and the members who agreed with him would cheer and the members who disagreed with him would hiss and boo and make derogatory remarks. Slab said it was almost as good as professional wrestling.

I asked him if he envisioned Montana having both a House of Lords and a House of Commons and he said if nothing else, the people we've been sending to Helena are common, so we would only need a House of Commons. He pointed out with only one House, we'd only have to send half as many people to Helena and would probably save enough money to give us all a tax cut.

Slab said if Montana adopted a Parliamentary form of government, and every day Governor Judy Martz appeared on the floor arguing for her programs, and there were a lot of cheers and boos, it would be worth televising. He also pointed out that Judy doesn't look like the type who would take kindly to being booed, so she might give some guy a knuckle sandwich, which would be great for the ratings.

I told him that up until now I had never been a big fan of Parliamentary government, but after listening to him, I might have to rethink my position.

'District Judge' – April 15, 2010

I saw my friend Slab Marble the other day and he asked if I'd noticed all of the yard signs sprouting up urging us to vote for various and sundry people who want to be a District Judge. I agreed it appears that almost everybody in the area is seeking the job, and since we are adding an additional judge, there is no incumbent.

Slab said he was thinking about running but he was told you had to have a law degree, which was obviously discriminatory, and was probably the reason it is so difficult to get good people like him to run for office.

I told him that they probably felt a legal background was necessary for someone who wanted to be a District Judge. Slab said he had pointed out to them that when he was in the army, he offered people so much free advice, he was often called a latrine lawyer. I said I was amazed that upon hearing that, the officials hadn't agreed to bend the rules a little and let him run. Slab said those were his sentiments exactly.

I then suggested that instead of trying for the office of District Judge, perhaps he should consider running for the job of Justice of the Peace since you are still sort of a judge, but you don't have to have a law degree. Slab asked what the qualifications were for that job, and I said I thought the primary requirement was that you had to have a pulse, and there are those who claim even that is more of a suggestion than a requirement.

He said he had his heart set on wearing a black robe and asked if he could wear one if he was a Justice of the Peace. I told him I thought some JP's wore black robes but on the other hand, I had heard of some who held the job of Justice of the Peace who dispensed justice while wearing their pajamas.

Slab said the more he learned about it, the more interested he was in the job, and he'd probably seek that office the next time around. He then asked if I would be willing to put one of his campaign signs up in my yard. I promised him a prime location, right out there with the dandelions.

'Beer Tax' – February 13, 2003

I had a call from my friend Slab Marble the other night and he sounded real agitated. Slab said that he understood Montana legislators were acting even goofier than usual and were now talking about putting a big tax on beer.

I told him that lawmakers were giving serious consideration to enacting a lot of sin taxes and that beer was one of the things that were on the sin list. Slab asked if this was going was going to include whatever beer is on sale this week, which is what he always buys. I told him I was quite certain they wanted to tax all beer.

Slab said he was really bummed and that if lawmakers wanted to raise some money there are a lot of other things that deserve to be taxed, and they should quit messing around with essential items such as whatever beer is on sale this week.

Against my better judgment, I asked him what the other things he thought should be taxed instead of his beer.

Slab said they should put a dollar a pound tax on liver. He said he hates liver and anything as gross as liver deserves to be taxed, and he also thought they should put a hefty tax on every can of Spam. I pointed out that some folks actually like Spam and he said if they'd been forced to dine on it seven days a week like he did when he was in the army, they'd all agree Spam should be heavily taxed.

I asked him if there was anything else he felt legislators should consider taxing. Slab said some of the things that came to mind were canned peas, prune juice, buttermilk, parsnips, and fruitcake. He said he didn't care for any of these things and as far as he was concerned, lawmakers could tax the heck out of them and he wouldn't even notice it.

Slab said he was planning to sit down and write lawmakers a letter telling them to get their act together, but first he was going to make a run to the grocery store and stock up on whatever beer is on sale this week, before those troublemakers in Helena decide to tax the stuff out of his price range.

I told him as usual, talking to him had been a mind boggling experience.

Chapter 7
SPORTS

"An outsider with a degree of objectivity would have asked, "Why are these idiots continuing to golf in weather like this?"

- Vic Miller

'Golf is Exercise' – April 13, 2000

I was reading an article in the local paper recently where a heart surgeon named Dr. John Pheifer who is visiting the state, was giving his views on how we should eat and exercise. They included cutting down on or even eliminating red meat from our diets if we want to live longer.

If Dr. Pheifer wants to live longer, I hope he doesn't express this view while participating in the cocktail hour in a saloon in a small town in the middle of cattle country.

However, the thing that really prompted me to question whether he really knows what he's talking about, is when he stated that while biking, walking, and swimming qualify as exercise, golf is not an exercise.

If Dr. Pheifer plays golf riding around the course in a golf cart while sipping some bottled water, I can understand why he doesn't think it is exercise. However, as a high handicapper who trudges around the course toting my own golf bag, I take exception to Dr. Pheifer's claim.

For example, while the scorecard might claim the course is 6,000 yards long, high handicappers can count on walking at least 12,000 yards during a round of golf. First, we slice the ball way off to the right, on the second shot we compensate for the slice and hook it to the left, the third shot hits a tree and lands 30 yards behind us after almost taking our head off on the way back. When we finally get close to the green, we blade the ball 15 yards past, before finally chipping it on. From there, we four putt as a result of hitting the first three putts way past the cup.

We have only played the first hole, which the scorecard claims is 392 yards, and have already walked more than 700 yards. Included in the total is a 50 yard dash running back to get the headcover we left in the fairway.

So, in spite of what Dr. Pheifer claims, golf is definitely exercise and if it wasn't for a good T-bone steak now and then, most of us would never be able to make it around the course.

Chapter 7 - Sports

'Olympics' – February 14, 2002

I encountered my friend Slab Marble the other day and asked him if had watched the opening ceremonies of the Winter Olympics down in Salt Lake.

Slab said even though he was still bummed because of the hanky panky that resulted in the Olympics ending up in Salt Lake instead of Red Lodge, he did decide to watch. He said they were so secretive about who was going to actually set the Olympic cauldron on fire that he was beginning to suspect it must be Mrs. O'Leary's cow, but it turned out to be the 1980 Olympic hockey team.

He then told me that NBC had invited Jim McKay, the ABC broadcast veteran to be a guest commentator, apparently not realizing he had been dead for two years. He said in spite of this they somehow managed to get Jim propped up on the set and he looked pretty good, although he talked kind of funny.

He then told me President Bush said a few words and while most of the judges gave him a 5.8, a couple gave him a zero. I told him they were probably the same ones who judge ice skating.

I asked Slab if he planned to watch a lot of Olympic coverage and he said he didn't think so, since it isn't as exciting as it was in the good old days, when the amateur participants were real amateurs.

He said he used to get all choked up at the sight of a downhill skier from Kuwait, wearing a snowmobile suit and a welder's helmet, coming down the ski run at about a hundred miles an hour, screaming at the top of his lungs as he realized he didn't have the faintest idea how to stop when he got to the bottom of the hill.

I agreed those were truly Olympic moments, and then asked Slab if Martha Stewart was at the Olympics this year. Slab said he hadn't seen her, and I told him she was at the winter Olympics four years ago, and there was some talk about having her come down the luge run on an ironing board as part of the closing ceremonies. Slab said if she planned on doing it this year, it's something he'd be sure to watch.

'Concussions' – November 19, 2010

I called my friend Slab Marble and asked him what he planned to do on Thanksgiving. Slab said he planned to stay home, eat about ten pounds of turkey and then turn on the TV and watch a bunch of guys, most of them about the size of a full grown buffalo, play football. He recalled that when he was younger he'd get together with a bunch of friends on Thanksgiving morning and they'd play two-hand touch football just to work up an appetite for the Thanksgiving feast, but he gave that up a few years ago when the day after Thanksgiving he tried to get out of bed and none of his moving parts wanted to move.

He then volunteered that given the fact the NFL commissioner is fining football players right and left for ringing each others bells, it wouldn't be long before he'd be watching two-hand touch football on television. But instead of a bunch of old out of shape dudes like himself, it would be touch football played by the guys who are the size of a full grown buffaloes.

I allowed he probably wouldn't be so critical of the commissioner if he knew anything about concussions. Slab said for my information he had bonked his noggin so many times he could write a book on concussions. He recalled that during one of his touch football games he was looking back over his shoulder in anticipation of catching a pass, ran into the goal post, and knocked himself out.

I asked if his friends were concerned that he might have a concussion and called an ambulance. Slab said no, when he came to, they just gave him a swig of cold beer, pointed out that watching him run into the goal post was one of the funniest things they'd ever seen, and hoped that he'd do it again sometime when they had a camera.

I told him that since Thanksgiving is a time for giving thanks, maybe before stuffing himself with turkey, he should pause and give thanks for the fact his touch football days ended before he got bonked on the head once too often and found himself announcing that he was going to be a candidate for the school board. Slab agreed that was something to be thankful for.

'Fitness' – November 1, 2000

I recently saw my old friend Slab Marble and he looked terrible. I asked him what in the world was wrong with him, and he said it was all because of his fitness program.

I told him I never associated him with fitness. Slab said that changed when he woke up one morning, looked into the mirror and was startled to see that his head was attached to John Madden's body. He said he decided then and there he was going to have to get in shape. He told me he decided to try jogging even though he'd never seen a jogger who looked all that happy.

I asked him if he went out and bought a pair of $200 running shoes. Slab said he figured combat boots must be the best thing for jogging since that's what the Army had him wear when they ran his tail off in basic training, and far be it for him to second guess the army. I inquired as to how the jogging worked out, and he said, not too well.

Slab told me when he dug out his old combat boots they pinched his feet, so his feet must have expanded along with the rest of his body. Then the first time out, the shoelace came untied on one of the boots and he tripped on it and landed on his face, smashing his nose. The second time out, two Dobermans chased him for five blocks, and on his third and final outing, he spotted an attractive young woman jogging on the other side of the street, and while watching her he ran into a power pole and smashed his nose again.

I said that at this point he must have had some second thoughts about getting in shape, and he admitted that he did, but decided to give it one more shot.

He said he noticed an ad for an exercise machine and sent away for it. About a week later, the UPS guy drove up, left the carton on the front step, and drove off. Slab told me he attempted to pick it up, only to discover it weighed over 200 pounds, and he ended up with a hernia. Now, he's barely able to walk, let alone exercise. He said at that point he decided quit trying to get in shape before he killed himself.

I told him that given his track record, it probably wasn't a bad idea.

Chapter 7 - Sports

'Soccer' – June 27, 2002

I went to see a Mustang game at Cobb Field and spotted my friend Slab Marble standing in the beer line. He complained to me their beer was kind of expensive compared to the stuff he usually drinks, and I told him that almost any liquid with the exception of water was more expensive than the stuff he usually drinks.

I then asked him if he had watched any of the soccer games featuring the United States in the World Cup. Slab asked if those were the games that took place in the middle of the night and I told him yes. He said the middle of the night is for sleeping, not watching a bunch of guys running around in their shorts, acting like demented gerbils.

I told him I was shocked that he hadn't been swept up by the emotion of the games since the good old U.S.A. enjoyed so much success. Slab said the way I was carrying on, they must have won the world Cup. I told him that no, but they almost made it to the semi-finals. Slab said big deal, and that he almost grew to be seven feet tall and only missed it by about a foot and a half.

I pointed out that while we didn't win the World Cup, just winning a couple of games was a big deal to soccer fans in this country but he apparently wasn't a big soccer fan. He said I had that right and that while soccer might be fun to play it was dull to watch, and he has a policy of never watching a soccer game unless a family member under the age of 12 is participating.

Slab said if I needed any proof that soccer is a dopey game, in baseball when Roger Clemens hits some guy in the noggin with a baseball it prompts a near riot, while in soccer, players go out of their way to have soccer balls bounce off their heads, and if that isn't dopey he doesn't know what is.

I said I gathered from our conversation that watching a soccer game on television was probably the last thing he would ever do. Slab told me it was actually the next to last. He said last thing he would ever do is turn on the TV and watch some guy trying to catch a fish.

Chapter 7 - Sports

'Summer Olympics' – October 8, 2009

I saw my friend Slab Marble the other day and asked him what he thought about all this fuss over the 2016 Summer Olympics. Slab said he hadn't been following the news recently since his TV set had given up the ghost. He said he was sitting there watching one of those reality television shows where some dimwit on an island was getting ready to eat something that appeared to be a dead muskrat and, all of a sudden, smoke started coming out of the TV and the picture disappeared. I told him maybe the reality television show was more than his old TV could take and Slab agreed that might have been the case.

He then told me he'd been shopping for a new television and didn't understand all this stuff about high definition but had just about decided to buy whatever was on sale that week, figuring if it worked for beer, it would probably work for television sets.

He then asked about the 2016 Summer Olympics, and I said that while the Obamas and Oprah Winfrey had made a trip overseas to try to convince the Olympic committee to select Chicago for the host city, the windy city got shot out of the saddle. Slab said it's too bad Al Capone isn't still alive since he'd have gone over and made the committee an offer they couldn't refuse. He then asked if the Olympic committee had selected Butte. I told him no, and he said that was a real shame since having the Summer Olympics in the Mining City would have been almost as big a deal as the annual St. Patrick's Day celebration.

Slab then said he hadn't planned on attending the Olympics anyway, and that he no longer even watches the Olympics on television. He said that, a number of years ago Martha Stewart was on hand for the Winter Olympics and a supermarket tabloid claimed she planned to come down the luge run on an ironing board. He said he kept tuning in and it never happened, so he has been boycotting the Olympics ever since. I told him he might want to watch the 2016 Summer Olympics since I understood a supermarket tabloid was now claiming Oprah Winfrey would be competing in the pole vault. Slab said that might be enough to make him tune in.

Chapter 7 - Sports

'Super Bowl Halftime Show' – February 1, 2001

I had a call from my friend Slab Marble and he opened the conversation by saying, "Did you ever see anything as pathetic in all your life?"

I told him that while I had heard some folks use the word dysfunctional when describing the Montana Legislature, I felt pathetic might be a bit harsh. Slab said this time it wasn't the goofy Legislature, but rather the Super Bowl that had him all bummed out. I reminded him most Super Bowl games give new meaning to the word dull, so he shouldn't have been surprised. Slab then told me he wasn't talking about the game, it was the halftime ceremonies, which he called a slap in the face to real NFL football fans like him.

I asked him to define a real NFL football fan, and he said it was a guy like himself who sat at home every Sunday with his shirt unbuttoned and shoes off, drinking whatever beer was on sale that week, watching any football game that was available and shouting at the television every time the referees make the wrong call.

I admitted that pretty well described him, but asked what that had to do with the halftime show? Slab told me when he heard there was going to be a great Super Bowl halftime show, he assumed it was going to be something a real NFL fan could relate to, such a tractor pull or a demolition derby.

While I was mulling that over, he said he went ballistic when he discovered the Super Bowl halftime consisted of a bunch of people he'd never heard of, jumping around on stage like they were demented. To make matters worse, they were singing weird songs that Johnny Cash wouldn't record on a bet. He said he spent more time shouting at the halftime show than he normally does at the referees.

Slab also said he hadn't seen so many flashing lights since the time he got picked up for going through a red light, and the sight of them brought back some bad memories. He claimed he'd been blindsided by the promos, and the halftime show should have been for diehard NFL fans, not MTV fans.

Slab said he was going to write a letter to the NFL and tell them if next year's Super Bowl halftime show didn't include either mud wrestling or a demolition derby, he was going to skip the entire Super Bowl, turn to the Public Television channel, and watch two insects mating.

I agreed if that threat didn't make them change their ways, nothing would.

'Club Championship' – May 24, 2012

The other day after a round of golf, some of us were discussing the worst weather conditions we'd over golfed in.

The one that came to mind for me occurred about a dozen years ago during the Laurel Golf Club championship. I would hasten to point out I was not in the championship flight which is reserved for real golfers. In addition to the championship flight, there are flights for those of us with lesser talents, including the flight for the uncertain, where I can usually be found.

In any event, in the late 90's the club championship was held on a day when it rained so hard I thought I was back in the Philippines.

I found myself trudging around the course with water running down my glasses and down the back of my neck and the grips of my golf clubs were so wet I had trouble hanging on to them when I swung.

In spite of this we kept on golfing. An outsider with a degree of objectivity would have asked, "Why are these idiots continuing to golf in weather like this?" The reason is simple. This was the men's club championship, not the women's club championship. Had it been the women's club championship the women would have probably concluded that, golfing in weather like this was really stupid, and departed for the clubhouse to have a martini.

However, it's a macho thing with male golfers. It's the same reason someone with a 36 handicap, while looking at a fairway that's about ten yards wide, will pull out his driver instead of using an iron. This dude will haul off and whack the ball so far into the rough that even if they called in the Montana National Guard and they searched all day they wouldn't be able to find the missing pellet.

Anyway, no one wanted to be the first guy to drop out, so we continued to slog along, much like the demented preacher in the movie "Caddyshack." Eventually we finished the round, managed to drag out waterlogged carcasses back to the clubhouse and had a couple of beers.

In looking back, it shouldn't have been called the Club Championship. It should have been called the Single Digit IQ Open.

'Professional Golfers' - October 24, 1991

I was watching a golf tournament on TV a while back and some of the players were shooting ten under par. This was kind of depressing since I have a seventeen handicap, which means that I normally shoot seventeen above par.

Then it occurred to me that it wasn't fair to judge my game on the basis of what professionals were shooting. They have a lot of advantages that us garden variety hackers don't have. I'd like to see how well they'd do playing under the same conditions we experience each weekend.

For starters, no caddies. They'd have to pack their own bags and wonder if the abdominal pain is just gas or a hernia. They would also be required to use the faded-out golf balls with strange sounding names that have been fished out of a pond or a ditch.

And no more of those yardage charts showing the exact distance to each pin. They would have to guess at the distance, aided only by a half-dead evergreen shrub that serves as the 150-yard marker, give or take a dozen yards. If they hit the ball into then boondocks, they'd have to go find it themselves, while trying to remember if rattlesnakes always rattled before they strike.

You've probably noticed that the professionals are used to having absolute quiet when they are putting and get real upset if someone moves or snaps a picture. I'd like to see how well they would do while crouching over four-and-a-half-foot putt, knowing there's a 50/50 chance that one of their playing partners is going to goose them with the flag stick.

Golf on TV would be a lot more interesting if the professionals played under the same conditions as those of us in the real golf world. I have a feeling that not too many of them would be shooting under par.

We might even discover that some of them are actually seventeen handicappers.

Chapter 7 - Sports

'Little League Baseball' – May 14, 2009

Back when the crust of the earth was cooling, Larry Petersen and I coached a Little League baseball team. Our games were played at Lissa Field, on the corner of Rimrock and Virginia Lane. Gene Lissa owned the property and the land is now a parking lot for MSU-Billings.

Lissa Field's main claim to fame is that both Dave McNally and Brent Musburger played Little League baseball there before moving on to other things. In the case of Dave, it was to be a pitcher in the major leagues, while Brent became a network sportscaster. Brent later told me that while Dave would be working on his curve ball, he would be chucking rocks at birds in a nearby tree, which may explain why they both ended up where they did.

Coaching 9 to 12-year-olds was interesting. At one game one of our nine-year-old players was scheduled to enter the game and play right field. I looked out and we didn't have a right fielder. I looked down and the boy was standing next to me. I asked him why he wasn't out in right field. He said he couldn't, because he had to go to the bathroom. I'll bet this never happened to Casey Stengel when he was managing the Yankees.

Anyone who is acquainted with Little League baseball knows that the start of the season attracts inclement weather like lottery winners attracts lost relatives. The official record for rainfall was the 36-inches that fell during a 24-hour period in the Philippines, but I am positive that it rained more than that during the third inning of a game we were attempting to play at Lissa. We were in the dugout treading water and attempting to gather up all the baseball gear, while at the same time trying to reason with an emotional 9-year old who insisted we keep our promise. We conceded we'd promised him he could play second base the next inning but unfortunately, there wasn't going to be a next inning. As I recall, second base had just floated past the dugout and was halfway down the block.

I retired from coaching Little League after three years. Larry sat out a few years, then came out of retirement and served another hitch. I hope that the second time around he remembered to purchase flood insurance.

Chapter 8
TRAVEL

"My GPS doesn't attempt to hide the fact it thinks it is dealing with someone who must have flunked the driver's test at least three times."

- Vic Miller

Chapter 8 - Travel

'Bicycles' – October 21, 1999

My wife and I recently decided to load up our bicycles and try out the new bike path in Billings. Loading a couple of bikes into the back of a sports utility vehicle is a very simple task if you happen to own a forklift or a crane. Otherwise it can be life threatening.

As you all know from your history class, the one you signed up for but rarely attended, it was around 1,000 BC, that an Egyptian named Shishnak invented the first bicycle. At the time there were no sports utilities vehicles around so Shisnak had no idea how difficult it would be load a bicycle into one of them. Had he known, I am sure he would have designed it in a way so that when attempting to load it, the front wheel wouldn't turn, causing the handlebar to poke you in the eye.

Shisnak as you will recall, came to an untimely end when he attempted to ride his bike down the side of a pyramid. While he did achieve a speed of 130 mph, a record that still stands for riding a bike down the side of a pyramid, the fact remains he creamed himself. The accident prompted the government to issue an edict stating that in the future, all bicycles would have to be equipped with brakes.

Anyway, my wife and I eventually got our bikes loaded and then unloaded and had a chance to try out the new bike path. Riding on the bike path has certain advantages over riding on Billing's streets. On the bike path there is less chance of getting hit by a semi, or being run over by a driver who is convinced that stop signs are merely something the city puts up for decorative purposes.

As I recall, the last time I was on a bicycle, Herbert Hoover was still president but as we have often been told, once you learn how to ride a bicycle, you never forget something or other. While I hadn't forgotten how to ride a bike, there were a number of things that I had forgotten. One of them was that when straining to pedal it up a steep incline, having a foot slip off a pedal can be a real character building experience, and can result in your walking funny for a period of time. I take some comfort in knowing I am still better off than Shisnak.

In spite of that mishap, we were very impressed with the new bike path and agreed it is a tremendous addition to the area. It is the end result of a lot of hard work by some people who had the vision and tenacity to take the project from a dream to a reality. The community owes them our thanks.

And just as soon as I quit walking funny, I intend to find out where they live, and thank each and every one of them.

'Canada Trip' – September 4, 2003

My wife and I recently played host to a group of folks who toured Canada. For those of you who might have dozed off when they were teaching geography, Canada is a rather large country that is located somewhere north of Great Falls. The people who live there are very pleasant and look a lot like us but have a strange way of pronouncing their words. Because of this it is sometimes difficult to understand what they are saying, although in all fairness, not as hard as trying to figure out what people who live in New Jersey are saying.

In any event we hosted the trip. I would hasten to point out that hosting a trip is a great deal different that being the tour guide and the reason we were hosting is that I was the one who cut the commercial inviting folks to visit Seattle, Victoria, Vancouver, Banff, Lake Louise, Jasper, Calgary and back to Billings. Fortunately for everyone concerned we had a professional tour guide who not only knew where we were going, but actually got us there and back.

It would be extremely foolhardy for me to ever act as a tour guide, given the fact I often have a great deal of trouble finding where I parked the car at the shopping center. If I ever started off for Canada as the tour guide for a group, the odds are we'd probably all end up in Tibet.

Another reason I am not cut out to be a tour guide is that tour guides are expected to finish the tour with the same number of people who began the tour. I have always felt that if you lost one or two along the way that was normal shrinkage, and they'd probably show up sooner or later.

The folks who signed up and went on the tour were really nice people as evidenced by the fact that when we saw a really big bear, none of the folks suggested we stop the bus to find out if the fellow passenger packing a carry-on bag the size of a hay bale could outrun the bruin.

My wife and I thoroughly enjoyed the trip that included two days on a train through the spectacular Canadian Rockies, and for my fellow travelers who asked if I was going to do a commentary on the excursion, the answer is I still have the matter under consideration.

Chapter 8 - Travel

'Oregon Trip' - September 27, 2001

My wife and I recently went on vacation and spent a week in the state of Oregon, whose motto is "Bring lots of money, spend it fast and then get out of here, since we don't want riff raff like you contaminating our environment."

To help you spend your money fast, at some places along the coast they charge $2.00 for a gallon of regular unleaded gasoline.

While the speed limit in Oregon is lower than that of Montana, you might be interested in knowing that Oregon drivers still drive fast, although not as fast as Oregon drivers drive when they are in Montana. A lot of Oregon drivers apparently feel speed limit signs are merely suggestions.

We spent a great deal of time next to the ocean and had an opportunity to walk the beaches and enjoyed some great seafood. We also played a couple rounds of golf, and I discovered that when I hit a golf ball at sea level, it didn't go as far as it does on my home course at Laurel. Given the fact my golf ball doesn't go all that far at Laurel, powering a drive past the ladies tee box was a challenge at times.

We saw a number of whales, although I can't swear we didn't just see the same whale a number of times. Perhaps a group of whales gather each morning and the leader says, "Herman, I've decided that today it will be your turn to swim up and down the coast, surfacing occasionally to blow some air and water." Herman will protest that he swam up and down the coast yesterday, and now it is Willy's turn. The leader will say that Willy is kind of stuffed up today and isn't capable of providing the kind of spout that tourists expect.

However, as a reward for having the duty for two days in a row, the leader will give Herman permission to surface near a small sailboat at the end of the day, slap his tail on the water real hard, and scare the dickens out of the people on the boat.

If you think this is a goofy theory, wait until I do the commentary I have been working on about the conversation two horses have while being pulled down a Montana highway at 70 mph in a horse trailer.

'Student Drivers' - June 26, 1997

This is the time of year when a lot of high school students are taking a driver's training course, where they presumably learn a number of things that will prove to be invaluable when they get their drivers licenses and become full-fledged drivers.

Things such as developing razor sharp reflexes so they can hit the horn 1/1000 of a second after the light turns green, to let the driver in front of them know they are holding up traffic.

And things such as driving down a street for 17 blocks with their left turn signal blinking all the way.

I assume people learn all of this stuff in a driver's training course, because God knows, it's obvious they learn it somewhere.

Back when the crust of the earth was cooling and I was a teenager, we didn't have access to drivers' training courses, so we had to learn to drive on our own.

This involved finding someone who was either courageous enough, or dumb enough, to be in the same vehicle with us while we attempted to learn how to drive.

As I recall, back then the concept of an automatic transmission hadn't made it over the continental divide, so we had to learn to drive while pushing in on the clutch and manually shifting gears or, in all too many instances, attempting to shift gears while forgetting to push in on the clutch.

Anyway, it was usually a very noisy experience involving a lot of grinding sounds, along with violent starts and stops.

Fortunately, we learned to drive on country roads where there was little or no traffic. If we managed to keep the vehicle on the road, we got an "A", and if we were able to keep the vehicle in the vicinity of the road and didn't tear out a mile of barb wire fence, it was usually good enough for at least a "D".

In watching some student drivers recently, I couldn't help but be impressed by how careful and courteous they were. At the same time, I was aware that this was probably the only time in their lives many of them will drive like this.

It's a safe bet that once they get a license and have access to a vehicle, their role model will no longer be the chauffeur from the movie "Driving Miss Daisy." The smart money is betting that it will be Burt Reynolds from the movie "Smokey and the Bandit."

Chapter 8 - Travel

'Winter in Yellowstone' – March 7, 2002

Some of the members of the Miller clan visited Yellowstone Park in late February, entering at the Gardiner entrance, driving through the park to Cooke City and then returning. If you haven't visited Yellowstone in the winter, it is an entirely different experience than a summer visit.

For one thing, you don't see very many people wandering around wearing shorts. If you do see one, it's a good idea to roll up the windows and lock the doors if they approach your vehicle.

On this trip we didn't check out Old Faithful or the park sewer system or any of the other things that occasionally erupt. We save that excitement for our summer visits.

We saw a lot of elk, buffalo, and coyotes. When wolves were first reintroduced in Yellowstone some folks predicted that the wolves would kill all of the coyotes. However, anyone who has lived in Montana or Wyoming for any length of time knows that coyotes are the ultimate survivors.

We saw three coyotes gathered around the remains of an elk that probably didn't die of old age. The coyotes were eating, and a flock of ravens and a couple of bald eagles were standing around waiting their turn, when all of a sudden the coyotes vacated the premises. A short while later a wolf showed up.

I don't recall if they mentioned it in the driver's manual, but when driving a car in Yellowstone Park and a herd of buffalo come marching down the highway on your side of the road, they have the right of way. This is especially true if you're driving a compact car, unless you want it to be even more compact.

There wasn't a great deal of snow at Mammoth and not much in most of the park. Cooke City had a lot of snow by prairie standards but not nearly as much as we have seen on previous trips. Hopefully, recent storms have given the park some needed snow.

The only snowmobiles we saw were in Cooke City. Unlike the West Yellowstone to Old Faithful stretch, the Mammoth to Cooke City portion of the highway doesn't allow snowmobiles. At this point I could jump right into the middle of the Yellowstone Park snowmobile controversy, but coyotes aren't the only critters who know when to cut and run.

Chapter 8 - Travel

'Airplane Trip – May 12, 2005

I ran into my friend Slab Marble the other day and he said he understood I'd taken another journey on an airplane. I told him my wife and I had recently gone to Washington, D.C. and it had been a great trip.

Slab asked if we flew first class and I told him that we flew the other class. I said that I assumed that an urban sophisticate like himself always flew first class and Slab said he didn't fly first class because he was afraid that with all that leg room he might fall asleep, slide off the seat and hurt himself.

I told him that wouldn't happen if he kept his seat belt fastened and Slab said keeping the seat belt fastened put too much pressure on his hernia. I asked him what caused the hernia and Slab said he acquired it on an airline trip. He said a woman came on board with a piece of carry-on luggage the size of a full grown water buffalo and attempted to stuff it into one of those little overhead storage compartments on the plane. Slab said he was taking all this in when, she looked at him and said that, if he was a real man he'd do this for her.

He said since his manhood was at stake, he hoisted up the bag and it weighed so much his eyes bugged out, something popped, and bingo, he had a hernia.

Slab said after five minutes of pushing and pounding he finally got the thing jammed into the overhead compartment and by this time the women was doing her laptop computer thing and didn't even bother to thank him. He said he sat down hoping the pain would subside when the baby in back of him started crying. Slab said the kid had a set of lungs that would make a Metropolitan Opera singer green with envy and the kid kept it up for the entire flight. He told me at one point its screeching was so high pitched he could hear the wine glasses cracking up in the first class section.

I told him that talking to him had been a very enlightening experience and asked him what he planned to do about the hernia. Slab said he had an appointment to see a faith healer next Tuesday.

Chapter 8 - Travel

'Australians' – March 11, 2004

Slab Marble called and said he couldn't believe what that guy from Australia did. I told him it was rather remarkable the way Australian golfer Craig Parry won the Doral Golf Tournament, and that it was exciting to watch the guy known as Popeye because of his huge forearms win the playoff by having his second shot go into the cup for an eagle.

Slab said an eagle might have been impressive but the Australian he was referring to ended up with a hole in one. I told him I didn't recall an Australian golfer getting a hole in one recently and Slab said it wasn't a golfer it was a handyman.

He said Australian Brad Shorten picked up a nail gun and fired a nail into his own head. I told Slab that given some of his spooky experiences with power tools I could see how he could relate to Mr. Shorten.

Slab said what happened is Brad was enjoying a few beers with some of his buddies after working on his house. The conversation turned to construction site accidents and Brad picked up a nail gun, pointed it at his head and pulled the trigger. He later explained he knew it wouldn't fire because he had turned off the compressor that fired the gun.

However, it did fire and Brad drove a 1 ¼ inch nail into his skull just behind the temple. Slab said the beers the Australians were drinking must be more potent than the whatever beer is on sale that he consumes, because after nailing himself Brad insisted it was no big deal and wanted to remove the nail with a pair of pliers.

Slab said his buddies talked him out of it and insisted he go to a hospital. It took neurosurgeons four hours to remove the nail from Brad's noggin but apparently the nail didn't hit anything vital. I pointed out that when your brain's the size of a walnut it's a rather small target but on the basis of what happened to both Craig Parry and Brad Shorten it is obvious that Australians are full of surprises.

Slab said they seem to be a couple of guys he'd enjoy having a beer with, although he might take a rain check if Brad was holding a nail gun. I told him that was good thinking.

'Cell Phones' – January 19, 2006

I decided to give my friend Slab Marble a call to see if his working parts were still working and as soon as he answered, he asked if I was calling on a cell phone. I told him that was a weird question and Slab said he was mad at cell phone users these days. I assured him I was not using a cell phone and asked what prompted the anti-cell phone crusade.

Slab said he was behind a car at a stop light and the guy in front of him was jabbering away on his cell phone. He said the light turned green and the clown was so involved in his phone conversation that he wasn't even aware the light had changed and sat there until the light turned red again.

I told Slab I had never considered him the shrinking violet type and asked why he hadn't leaned on his horn to remind the guy the light was green. He said he'd been having some problems with the electrical system on his 1964 Cadillac and every time he honks the horn, his car radio switches to a religious station and somebody starts preaching at him.

I said I could see where that could be upsetting, but pointed out he might be overreacting since having to sit through a traffic light change wasn't the end of the world. Slab said maybe not for me, but given the price of gas and the fact his Caddy only gets about seven miles to the gallon, having to sit through traffic light changes costs him real money.

He said the next time the legislature has one of those not all that special sessions, they should pass a law about this, and it should have teeth in it. Maybe stating that anyone who disrupts traffic flow by blabbering on a cell phone at a traffic light causing pain and suffering to another driver will be forced to serve a full term on a school board. I told him I thought that was a bit harsh but Slab said desperate times call for desperate measures and its obvious traffic crimes are escalating. He pointed out we already had the lawless element who don't wait their turn at four way stop intersections. I told him he'd convinced me and I'd contact my legislator right away.

'Diagonal Parking' – August 15, 2002

I was taking a stroll in downtown Billings recently and saw my old friend Slab Marble standing on the sidewalk shaking his head. I asked him what was causing him to be perplexed and he told me the moon must be in the wrong place. He said for years, no one seemed to have that much of a problem with diagonal parking and now all of a sudden half of the drivers in the downtown area are attempting to parallel park, then giving up and abandoning their vehicles.

I told him he had it all wrong and people were parking this way on purpose because someone decided it would be nice if we had both parallel parking and diagonal parking.

Slab asked if this was the same person who came up with the idea of spending hundreds of thousands of dollars to put up the goofy looking thing at the downtown intersection and I said I didn't know.

I told him that his problem was he always resisted change. He denied it and said it was just that his 1964 Cadillac had enough dings in it without someone coming up with a dopy plan that was likely to cause bodily harm to both the car and himself. He said with his luck he'd find himself with a huge van on each side of him and he'd back out in front of an oncoming cement truck and get himself creamed.

I said it was just like him to be thinking of himself instead of the welfare of downtown Billings, pointing out a lot of time and money had been spent to make the area more exciting. Slab said it was going to be exciting all right, particularly in the winter when the streets were slick and there were all these crashing sounds followed by the sound of a lot of sirens.

I told him he was being too negative and that he of all people didn't have to worry about anyone hitting him while he was backing out of a diagonal parking space. I pointed out that no one in their right mind is going to risk a collision with a 1964 Cadillac with a lot of dings and has a bumper sticker reading, "LIABILITY INSURANCE? WHAT'S THAT?"

Slab said those were comforting words and now he felt a lot better about diagonal parking.

Chapter 8 - Travel

'Parking Garage' – June 20, 2013

I saw my friend Slab Marble and mentioned that I understood they are going to build a new stud muffin parking garage in downtown Billings.

Slab said he has never been a big fan of parking garages because on the one occasion when he tried to use one it didn't have a happy ending. He said it started out when a contraption issued him a claim ticket. He said he immediately started worrying about losing it and not being able to get his 1964 Cadillac out of there without hiring a lawyer.

He then went on to say there were all of these parking spaces but he is obviously one of the unwashed masses and not allowed to park there since these spots were reserved for people who are higher on the food chain.

He said by the time he had driven round and round until finally reaching the part of the garage where clods like him were allowed to park, the people on the street below looked to be the size of ants. Slab then told me he thought because of the altitude he was suffering from oxygen deprivation because the parking spaces looked to be about the size of the army cot he had when he was in the army, but unfortunately it wasn't just an illusion.

When he pulled into one, the vehicles on either side of him were so close he couldn't get his car door open and the only possible escape route was through the trunk, so at that point he gave up, left the parking garage and drove back home.

He said he hoped when they build the new parking garage they'll make the spaces large enough so you can not only park the vehicle but actually get out of the vehicle.

I told him that was an interesting, if somewhat radical thought.

Chapter 8 - Travel

'Cadillac Smoke' – May 21, 2009

The other day I noticed a big cloud of smoke at the other end of our street. It was a scene reminiscent of that old movie where they had all of those smudge pots going in a fruit orchard in an attempt to save the crop from a big frost. Then I realized that the smoke was coming from the exhaust pipe of a 1964 Cadillac driven by my friend Slab Marble. He pulled into our driveway and after the smoke had cleared, I mentioned that his vehicle appeared to be burning a little oil. Slab admitted that while the Caddy gets about 10 miles on a gallon of gasoline, it only gets about 5 miles on a quart of oil.

I asked if he'd heard that President Obama wants all new cars sold in 2016 get 39 miles per gallon of gas. Slab said in 2016 he still plans on driving his Caddy, and the only time it gets 39 miles per gallon is when it's being towed.

He told me he has replaced just about everything on the car with junkyard parts, with the exception of the turn signals, which have never been used. He said he figures making a turn is a personal thing, and it's nobody else's business. Slab then informed me that he had worn out three horns, honking at idiot drivers who don't wait their turn at four way stop intersections.

He volunteered that he does most of his own mechanic work since he has lots of tools. I said I was aware of that, and most of those tools are ones that he has borrowed from me and never returned. Slab said anytime I wanted to borrow one to just stop by.

I said that was very generous of him, but since he obviously hadn't stopped by to return my tools, he must have something else on his mind. Slab said he just happened to be in the neighborhood and while he usually travels with a case of oil in the trunk, he remembered he'd forgotten to do that, and wanted to know if I could loan him a couple of quarts of oil so he could make it back home.

I said I'd be happy to. Since he hadn't asked to borrow more tools, I figured I got off easy.

Chapter 9
WHERE ANGELS FEAR TO TREAD

"I seem to have misplaced last year's predictions...
however, we are not here to dwell on the past,
but rather to squint into the future."

- Vic Miller

Chapter 9 - Where Angels Fear to Tread

'1997 Predictions' – January 9, 1997

It is traditional for me to begin the year with my "Where Angels Fear to Tread" predictions. For those of you who don't recall last year's predictions, I would like to tell you that I was 100% correct. For those of you who do recall last year's predictions, so I missed a few. Big deal!!

However, I am not here to dwell on the past, so here are my predictions for 1997.

House Republicans will announce that Newt Gingrich will resign as House Speaker and will be assuming his new duties as a restroom attendant at the Capitol. All concerned will deny this is a demotion.

Hillary Rodham Clinton will be indicted for attempting to sell the White House to a wealthy Asian businessman, who reportedly planned to convert it into a sauna and massage parlor.

Asked to comment on this, President Clinton will say he doesn't recall ever meeting anyone named Rodham, but with so many people coming and going at the White House, he can't be expected to remember all of them.

At the Montana Legislature, lawmakers, after ignoring the problem for years, will finally deal with the fact that the meadowlark goes south every winter and determine that Montana deserves more than a part time state bird. They will make this the top priority of the session. The "Montana Deserves More Than a Part Time State Bird" subcommittee will meet and designate the black capped chickadee, a year-round resident of the state, as the new state bird.

Unfortunately, at the same time in a room next door, the "Let's Find Something New to Shoot" subcommittee will meet and designate the black capped chickadee a game bird. They will then establish a chickadee-hunting season to run between January 1 and December 31, with a daily bag limit of five.

The number two priority of the session will be the issue of a speed limit for Montana. One side will insist on a speed limit of 35 mph, while the other side will be equally insistent that the speed limit be 135 mph. In the spirit of compromise, lawmakers will determine that, effectively immediately, the daytime speed limit will be 35 mph while the nighttime limit will be 135 mph.

Lawmakers will then announce they are leaving Helena and will spend the remainder of the session down south, notifying meadowlarks that they have been fired.

It could be a long year.

Chapter 9 - Where Angels Fear to Tread

'2000 Predictions' - December 30, 1999

It is time once again for Miller's annual "Where Angels Fear to Tread" predictions for the coming year. For any troublemakers out there who want to know how I did last year, let's just say I did as well as a lot of those prima donna baseball players who get paid millions of dollars for striking out.

Following bitter partisan arguments about what to do with the purported general fund surplus in Montana, officials will open the state vault. They will discover the only thing in there is two expired Lotto tickets and a letter from Publishers Clearinghouse saying, "you could be the next winner of $10,000,000!"

Robert Fulghum, who wrote the book "All I Really Need to Know I Learned in Kindergarten" will announce he is moving to Montana and will be a candidate for the office of Superintendent of Public Instruction. He will run on a platform of abolishing all education past kindergarten, thus saving Montana taxpayers millions of dollars. Fulghum will win by a landslide and immediately become the frontrunner for the Reform Party presidential nomination.

The U.S. Department of Transportation will chastise Montana for not spending federal aid for highway construction funds fast enough. The desperate Montana Highway Department will announce plans to build a new billion dollar six lane interstate highway between Billings and Molt. The project will include palatial rest stops located every quarter mile along the way.

And finally, there has been a lot of speculation as to what Governor Marc Racicot will do when he leaves office. Many have predicted a cabinet post if George W. Bush is elected president.

Newly elected George W. Bush will announce that he is going to nominate Marc Racicot to be the next Pope. An angry Vatican spokesman will say it is out of the question, pointing out that it is the cardinals, not the President of the United States who select the Pope.

President Bush will ask the spokesman how many nuclear weapons the cardinals have. The spokesman will then say, come to think of it, the cardinals always burn their ballots and all that smoke coming out of the chimney probably causes air pollution. A statement will be released stating that everyone at the Vatican is looking forward to the arrival of Pope Marc.

At this point I know what a lot of you are probably thinking, and a Happy New Year to you too.

'2002 Predictions' – December 27, 2001

It is time once again for my Where Angels Fear to Tread" predictions for the coming year. As is usually the case I seem to have misplaced last year's predictions, but I am almost certain I didn't miss on any of them. However, we are not here to dwell on the past, but rather to squint into the future.

Activists will beat the bushes and get enough signatures to have a number of issues placed on the November ballot. Among them will be a proposal for the state to buy all of the Montana Power Company dams, with the stipulation they can not produce energy, but must be set aside for the exclusive use of snowmobilers in the summer. Another would impose a $1,000 fine on anyone driving more than one block with the left turn signal blinking, a third would make jaywalking the official state dance in Montana, and last but not least, a proposal to do away with the legislature and replace it with three guys named Earl.

The Montana Supreme Court, in a 5-2 decision, will rule that when Montana Vigilantes apprehended and hanged famous road agent Henry Plummer in 1864, they failed to read him his Miranda rights. The court will order the State of Montana to spend as much money as necessary to do a total reclamation project on him and restore him to his original state.

In a poll taken by people who are always taking polls, when asked to name the Lt. Governor of Montana, respondents will be almost evenly split. 51 % of those responding will say it's Dan Quayle, with 49% reasonably certain it's Harry Potter.

And while we are on the subject of polls, after several polls show Governor Judy Martz with low approval ratings, the Governor will go to court and have her name legally changed to Marc Racicot.

All in all, it shapes up as a year when it might be a good idea to hide under the bed, but before you do, I'd like to take this opportunity to wish you a Happy New Year.

Chapter 9 - Where Angels Fear to Tread

'2003 Predictions' – December 26, 2002

Now that we have managed to thrash another perfectly good year, it is time to look ahead to 2003. For a number of years, I have devoted one of these commentaries to my "Where Angels Fear to Tread Predictions" for the upcoming year, and I'm not one to mess with tradition, so away we go.

Secretary of Defense Donald Rumsfeld, expanding on his previous claim that the United States is capable of fighting wars in any number of geographical locations at the same time, will announce that unless Guam changes its ways, we will send an aircraft carrier over there and launch an attack. When someone points out that Guam is a possession of the United States, Mr. Rumsfeld will claim he was misquoted, and the warning was actually aimed at Canada.

Senator Trent Lott, upset over the fact he was given the bums rush by the GOP, will announce that he is giving serious consideration to switching parties. He will immediately become the frontrunner for the Democratic presidential nomination.

Alan Greenspan will appear before a congressional committee and solemnly announce that in 2003 the nation's economy will get better, unless it gets worse. The stock market will react to this news by throwing up.

Here in Montana, Governor Judy Martz, in her State of the State Address, will tell a joint session of the Montana House and Senate that Montana is a state and as long as she is Governor, it will remain a state. Democrats will accuse her of lying.

The Montana Legislature, faced with huge budget deficits, will introduce 25,000 new bills, none of them having anything to do with the budget deficit.

However, in the closing days of the session, lawmakers, in an effort to get the state on sound financial footing, will vote to tap the coal tax fund to the tune of $300-million and use the money to buy Baghdad Power and Light Company stock.

And stung by criticism that the state had done little to prepare for the thousands of visitors expected for the upcoming Lewis and Clark bicentennial, state tourism officials will angrily deny the claim, pointing out they have signed an agreement to lease two portable toilets, one to be placed in western Montana and the other in eastern Montana.

And there you have it, another year to look forward to.

Chapter 9 - Where Angels Fear to Tread

'2004 Predictions' – January 8, 2004

Ready or not, it's time once again for our annual "Where Angels Fear to Tread" predictions for the coming year.

When polls show that an unnamed Democratic candidate would run better against President George Bush than any of the named Democratic presidential candidates, all of the Democratic presidential candidates will go to court and ask to have their names legally changed to Unnamed Democratic Candidate.

In the November election, nine out of ten Florida voters will get confused and write in the name "Pregnant Chad" as their choice for president.

In spite of coming in second to "Pregnant Chad" in the state of Florida, President George Bush will be able to get enough electoral votes to win his second term as president. In his State of the Union address he will announce that after concluding there were too many states in the union, he has sold the state of New York to Donald Trump.

Hillary Rodham Clinton, when informed that she is now the senator of a non-existent state, will announce that, given the fact her favorite song has always been "Stand By Your Man", will move to Nashville and become a country music singer.

On Wall Street, the Dow Jones industrial average will continue to be about average. Meanwhile, NASDAQ, in an effort to get more people to invest, will change its name to POWERBALL.

Here in Montana, Democratic gubernatorial candidate Brian Schweitzer will announce that after interviewing everyone in the state in his search for a running mate, he has decided to have himself cloned and be his own running mate.

Political pundits will hail this as a brilliant political move, but in the end it won't be enough to get him elected. In the greatest upset in the history of Montana politics, Bob Kelleher, running for the one hundredth time, will win the election by two votes. Kelleher will immediately abolish the legislature and replace it with a Parliamentary form of government with him as the new Prime Minister.

He will also reveal his plan to have the statue of Thomas Meagher removed from in front of the Capitol building and replace it with a statue of Margaret Thatcher. Unfortunately, at the dedication ceremony, former governor Judy Martz will accidentally back over the new statue with a garbage truck. And there you have it, another vintage year in the offing.

Chapter 9 - Where Angels Fear to Tread

'2010 Predictions' – December 30, 2009

Now, the moment all of you have been dreading. My annual "Where Angels Fear to Tread" predictions for the coming year.

Archeologists will do a further examination of the skeleton of Lucy, a woman who lived on earth over three million years ago, and discover that she was wearing an engagement ring given to her by West Virginia Senator Robert Byrd.

While in the White House Rose Garden, President Obama will trip over a rose bush and land on his head. During the 30 seconds that Mr. Obama is unconscious, Vice President Joe Biden will order all American troops to return from Iraq and Afghanistan, saying they will be needed here, given the fact he has just declared war on Canada.

Tiger Woods will issue a press release admitting that in addition to his other transgressions, after missing the cut in the 2009 British Open, he was depressed and began an intense relationship with Britain's Queen Elizabeth.

The city of San Francisco, a community in the forefront of enlightened thinking, will pass a law banning marriage between heterosexuals.

The administration and members of Congress will devote almost all of their waking hours thinking up new ways to spend money, but in spite of this, the budget deficit will continue to increase. A deeply concerned President Obama will name Bernie Madoff to be the new Treasury Secretary.

Senator Max Baucus will hold a press conference and announce that, after looking back on 2009, both he and Tiger Woods have decided they are going to ask if they can take a mulligan.

Two Montana legislators will claim they were victims of blatant discrimination since they were the only two Democrat lawmakers who weren't appointed to state jobs by either Governor Brian Schweitzer or State Auditor Monica Lindeen. Governor Schweitzer's brother Walt will claim the two lawmakers are the same malcontents who refused to buy tickets from him when he was raffling off the Governors Mansion.

Finally, a team exploring a remote valley in Silver Bow County will come across a tribe of people long thought to be extinct. Genetic tests will determine that these people are indeed descendants of an ancient tribe that once lived in the Butte area before disappearing about a thousand years ago. They were known as Republicans. And there you have it, another fun filled year in the offing.

LAST ON-AIR COMMENTARY

"There's a time to charge, and a time to retreat."
- Vic Miller

'Last On-Air Commentary' – December 26, 2013

This will be my last television commentary as I wrap up a six-decade broadcasting career. I have observed too many instances where someone has stayed too long at the ball and have no desire to add to the list.

I have done hundreds of commentaries, often marching to the beat of a different drum, and at no time was I told what to say. Almost all of the material I've used has come from my own warped mind and on those occasions where I used someone else's material I have attempted to credit the source.

In looking back, it has been a good run starting on that October day in 1953 when I showed up at KOOK radio for my first day at work. Later, after moving over to KOOK TV, I had the opportunity to interview a U.S. President, Vice Presidents, Senators, Governors, and a host of celebrities. I just happened to be in a profession where those things happen.

I have had an opportunity to work for and with some tremendous people including the broadcasters I share the news set with tonight. I am deeply indebted to Joe Sample for everything he did for me during the three decades that he owned the station, and I was privileged to be the General Manager of KOOK TV/KTVQ for 18 of those years. If I began to name all of the folks, I've enjoyed working with it would take up the entire newscast.

I do want to thank my family, especially my wife JoAnne for their great support over the years, and my friend Slab Marble and I appreciate those viewers who were nice enough to tell me they enjoyed what we were doing.

As far as my future plans, I will probably follow the example of my friends from the Home for the Uncertain and start writing incoherent letters to the editor with a lot of misspelled words.

ABOUT THE AUTHOR

Vic was born and raised in White Sulphur Springs, Montana. Following graduation and a year at a radio broadcasting school in Seattle, he spent two years in the Army during the Korean conflict.

Vic began his broadcasting career in 1953 with KOOK radio in Billings, Montana as an announcer and newscaster. In 1959, he moved to KOOK TV (now KTVQ) and worked as a news anchor, operations director, and served as general manager of the station for 18 years. After his retirement in 1999, he continued to write and present commentaries for the KTVQ viewers until 2013.

He has been active in both broadcasting and community service having been the past president of the Montana Broadcasters Association and downtown Billings Rotary Club. Vic was a member of Montana Task Force studying political campaign reform, was a member of governing board of Montana Mathematics Coalition, and spent six years on the Eastern Montana College Executive Board. Additionally, he served numerous years on the boards of the Laurel Golf Club, Montana State University Billings Foundation, Yellowstone Kiwanis Club, Montana Energy Share, Senior Citizens Advisory Council, and Zoo Montana.

His many professional awards and community recognition include:

- Named 1994 Montana Media Advocate of the Year by the Small Business Administration
- Member of the Greater Montana Foundation Board of Trustees from 2000-2017
- Inducted into the Montana Broadcasters Hall of Fame in 1998
- Recipient of J.C. Penny Golden Rule Award for community volunteer service
- Boys and Girls Club Service to Youth Award
- Recipient of the first annual Chancellor's Award from Montana State University-Billings
- Distinguished Service Award from Rocky Mountain College.

Vic and his wife, JoAnne celebrated their 50-year wedding anniversary in 2006. They have two grown sons Gregory Miller and Bruce Miller (Sylvia Medina) and three grandchildren, Victor, Takara, and Tiago Miller.

KTVQ station retirement photo featuring a personalized message from CBS legendary broadcaster Walter Cronkite and signed by coworkers of KTVQ-2 television station.
Presented on July 30, 1999

Photo of the past presidents of the Montana Broadcasters Associations. (Vic is 3rd from the left in the back row).

Celebration party commemorating the last episode of the CBS television series M*A*S*H*
(Mobile Army Surgical Hospital) that ran from September 17, 1972 to February 28, 1983.
(Vic is the 2nd from the left in the back row).

Montana Broadcasters
Award for Distinguished
Service
Presented on June 11, 1976.

Service Award commemorating 40 years of service to KTVQ-2 television station and the Billings community.
Presented October 9, 1993.

Montana State University 1995 Chancellor's Award presented for years of distinguished professional and personal service, dedication, commitment, and support of the University and Foundation of Montana State University-Billings. Presented by the Chancellor, Dr. Ronald Sexton.

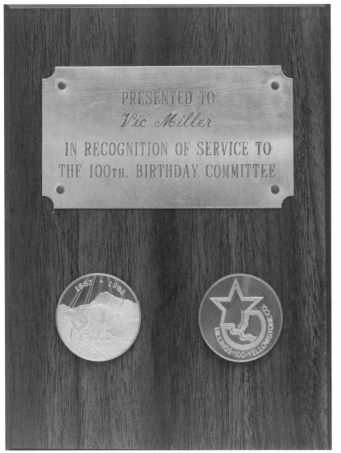

Award in recognition for service to the Billings, Montana 100th Birthday (1882-1992) Committee.

Vic Miller as an announcer
and newscaster at
KOOK radio
in Billings, Montana
in the mid 1950s.

JUNE 25
1996

Presented to

VICTOR MILLER

In appreciation for your dedicated
service to the Board of Governors of
the Montana Business Connections.

Service Award
from the Board of
Governors of the
Montana Business
Connections.
Presented
June 25, 1996.

Two of the original logos for the Montana Television Network (MTN) established in 1969 in
its current form by Montana broadcasting pioneer Joe Sample.

MTN was originally conceived as a way to unify Montanans and connect the state's
comparatively isolated population centers. The stars represent the MTN CBS affiliate stations
located in Billings (KOOK-TV, then KTVQ), Great Falls (KRTV), Butte (KXLF),
and Missoula (KPAX), Montana.

Starting in 1959, Vic Miller served as news anchor, operations director and station general
manager, a position he held for 18 years until retiring in 1999.

CITY OF BILLINGS
JAMES W. VAN ARSDALE
MAYOR
P.O. BOX 1178
BILLINGS, MT 59103
PHONE (406) 657-8296

P R O C L A M A T I O N

WHEREAS - VIC MILLER has observed the Montana scene for upwards of 50 years and has commented with accuracy and insight on that scene; and

WHEREAS - VIC MILLER brings humor and wit, an even temper, and a high moral standard to his commentaries and his life; and

WHEREAS - VIC MILLER delivers his commentaries in "rich, chocolate" tones so that women fans have said they "could listen to him all day," and lives his life in such a way that his peers consider him "class all the way;" and

WHEREAS - VIC MILLER has been active in the community, serving on boards for the Salvation Army and the United Way; as president of Rotary and the Montana Broadcasting Association; as an active member of Yellowstone Kiwanis; and as a Little League Coach; and

WHEREAS - VIC MILLER has maintained close ties with Eastern Montana College which his children and his wife have attended; and

WHEREAS - VIC MILLER served for 12 years as a member of the Local Advisory Board for Eastern Montana College and has always presented the college to the community in a positive fashion and supported it even when his position on the executive board was not a "fun spot" to be.

NOW, THEREFORE, I, JAMES W. VAN ARSDALE, MAYOR of the City of Billings, Montana, do hereby proclaim October 10, 1989, as

VIC MILLER DAY IN BILLINGS

and urge our community to pay special tribute to one of Billings' most outstanding citizens!

JAMES W. VAN ARSDALE, MAYOR

Proclamation by Billings Mayor James Van Arsdale
of Vic Miller Day
in Billings Montana, October 10, 1989.

Photo of Vic & JoAnne Miller at
Vic's KTVQ television station
retirement celebration,
July 30, 1999.

Printed in the USA
CPSIA information can be obtained
at www.ICGtesting.com
LVHW071724301023
762119LV00062B/949

* 9 7 8 1 9 5 5 0 2 3 1 5 3 *